Spiritual Warfare Ministries
Presents

# THE WEAPONS
# OF OUR
# WARFARE

## Volume I

### by Kenneth Scott

*(For the weapons of our warfare are not carnal, but mighty through God to the pulling down of strong holds;) Casting down imaginations, and every high thing that exalteth itself against the knowledge of God, and bringing into captivity every thought to the obedience of Christ.*

*2 Corinthians 10:4-5*

All Scriptures in this publication are taken from the King James version of the bible or paraphrased by the author.

*The Weapons Of Our Warfare* is a registered trademark of Spiritual Warfare Ministries, Inc., Birmingham, Alabama.

Third Edition of Volume I

The Weapons Of Our Warfare volume I
ISBN: 0-9667009-2-9
Copyright © 2001 by Spiritual Warfare Ministries, Inc.

# Contents

# Contents Continued

# Acknowledgment

*Special thanks to my bishop and his wife, Bishop Nathaniel and Valerie Holcomb, of the Christian House of Prayer Ministries in Copperas Cove, Texas, for their love, understanding and support. And, through whose anointed teaching and preaching of the Gospel, inspired this book to be written, so that others may learn how to be more effective in prayer warfare.*

# *Foreword*

When a person becomes a Christian, they instantly become part of a constant warfare with Satan. It's not a warfare where guns, bullets, or bombs are used, but a spiritual warfare. It's a warfare where life does not end with physical death, but rather, eternal death, or "Eternal Glory."

In the United States Army, soldiers are given various weapons and trained on how to effectively use them against the enemy. If they learn well, and use the weapons the way they were intended, each soldier has a very good chance of survival on the battlefield.

In the spiritual warfare against the powers of darkness, God has given us, as soldiers of Christ, powerful weaponry and defense. The other side does not have, nor can they ever develop a defense strong enough to defend against our weapons. As Christians, Jesus Christ dwells within us, giving us power and knowledge in the usage of our weaponry, as well as how to employ our defense tactics. As we use our weapons (by praying, believing and confessing the Word of God through the power and anointing of continual prayer), we destroy our enemy, his defense is broken down, and God gives us insurmountable victory over the devil and his works.

This book, "*The Weapons of Our Warfare*," is composed of dynamic, powerful, scriptural, and anointed prayers that will help you to become more effective in your warfare and battles against the devil. It is designed to aid and assist the believer in prayer. The words of these prayers are composed entirely of the sword of the Spirit, which is the Word of God. The various scriptures used in each prayer are focused to meet or address the specific needs of each prayer. Because, unless you use the right weapons, at the right time, for the right battle, you will not be able to defeat the enemy.

The scriptural references after each prayer are to assist you further. They are listed in order of the prayer so that you may be able to follow along with them to see how each prayer was formed and prepared from scripture.

You are encouraged to confess and pray these prayers until they become a part of you, and a part of your prayer life. As you continue to pray and confess these prayers, you will begin to see changes in the things you pray for, as well as experience the power of God throughout your life and your circumstances.

# Introduction

## I.  *How Prayer Works*

To understand how prayer works, let me give you an illustration. One day a mother and her son went to a large department store. While in the store, the child saw an interesting toy and asked his mother if he could have it. The mother told him that she could not get it for him at that time, but promised to get it for him the next time she came to the store. Several weeks later, the mother took another trip to the department store with her son. The son then reminded his mother that she had promised to get the toy for him the next time they came to the store. The mother, knowing that she had to keep her word, went ahead and bought the toy for her son.

This is an example of how prayer works. Every blessing in the bible is a promise that God has made to every born again believer. As the mother made and fulfilled her promise to her son in the illustration above, we remind God of His promises through praying and confessing the Word of God. As we do so, He keeps His Word and grants our petitions. In order for us to be effective in our prayer life, we must practice according to 2 Timothy 2:15, *"Study to show thyself approved unto God, a workman that needeth not to be ashamed, rightly dividing the Word of truth."*

We must study the Word of God in order to know the promises that are provided for us. If the son had reminded his mother of a different promise that his mother made him, he would not have received the toy. He had to remind his mother of the right promise in order for him to receive the toy.

## II.    *How To Apply The Word Of God Through Prayer*

Many people believe that when it comes to praying that we should just say what's on our heart. However, that's not the way Jesus instructed us to pray. In Luke 11:1, one of Jesus' disciples asked Him to teach them how to pray. Jesus did not tell them to simply say what was on their hearts; He gave them spiritual principles and guidelines by which to pray, resulting in what we all know as *"The Lord's Prayer."*

In Isaiah 43:26, God instructs us to put Him in remembrance of His Word. God is not senile in that He cannot remember what He has said, but He has established rules and guidelines for us to pray. Putting Him in remembrance of His Word is one of these guidelines. God does not need us to remind Him of the promises and blessings He has made us in His Word. But when we put Him in remembrance of His Word (by saying what His Word says), it increases our faith to believe and also receive what God has said.

A good example of this principle is that of the child reminding his mother of her promise. Since his mother made him the promise, the little boy had faith enough to believe that the next time they came to the store he would receive the toy.

Another reason why it is important for us to confess and pray the Word of God is because it releases the angels of God to bring the blessings of God to us. It also releases the power of God to act upon what we have prayed. In Psalms 103:20 it tells us that *"...angels harken to the voice of God's Word..."* If we do not speak God's Word, the angels have no authority to move out and bring our blessings.

As you pray the prayers in this book, they will provoke faith in your heart, and they will release the power of God upon His Word to act upon your prayers and bring them to pass.

## III.    *Speak Those Things That Be Not As Though They Were*

As you read and confess the prayers in this book, it may seem that these prayers do not completely apply to your specific situation.

*For example:*

You may be believing God to bless your finances, and part of your confession may be that you are the lender and not the borrower, and that you are above only and not beneath in your finances.

*Another example:*

A wife may be having problems in her marriage with her husband, and part of her prayer and confession over him may be that her husband is a man of God, one that loves his family, and one that leads and teaches them in the ways of the Lord.

Now in reality, the above confessions could be the furthest things from the truth concerning your situations and circumstances as they presently exist. However, in the latter part of Romans 4:17, it reads:

*...even God, who quickeneth the dead, and "<u>calleth those things which be not as though they were.</u>"*

God is saying that regardless of the condition of your circumstances, call (or pray and confess) those things which are not the way you desire or need them to be, as though they were the way that you desire or need them to be; because in the spiritual realm, they are already that way.

You see, before the world actually existed, God spoke those things which were not, as though they were, and they came to pass. God has given us that same power and authority to speak to our circumstances. All the promises of His Word exists for us in the spiritual realm, such as power in Christ Jesus, good health, long life, success, prosperity, love, peace, harmony, and so forth; and as we continually pray and confess the Word of God over our circumstances and situations in life, we bring the blessings of God which exist in the spiritual realm into the natural manifestation.

Regardless of how much it may seem that your circumstances are not in line with these prayers (or the Word of God), continue to pray and confess what God has said in His Word, instead of confessing the way things look. As you continue to *"speak those things which be not as though they were,"* those things will become manifested, and you will begin to see changes throughout your life and circumstances.

## IV.        *Making Prayer Personal*

Making prayer personal is another principal we must follow if we are going to be effective in our prayers. In the beginning of this book we discussed how every soldier has been given weapons with which to fight. The unique part of our warfare is that God allows us to use all the weapons He has made available to us in His Word.

### *For example:*

In Isaiah 53:5, God told Isaiah of the prophecy about the coming of Jesus Christ. In this prophecy, God lets Isaiah know that by the stripes that Jesus Christ would bear prior to the cross, they would enable him to be healed. This promise not only applied to Isaiah, it also applies to every born again believer.

*Another example:*

In 3 John 1:2, John was under the anointing of the Holy Spirit and wrote a letter to an elder name Gaius. He encouraged him by saying, *"Beloved, I wish above all things that thou mayest prosper and be in health, even as thy soul prospereth."*

Even though John wrote the letter, it was God, through him, inspiring the words to be written. In this scripture God was saying three things he desires for us:

1. God wants us to prosper spiritually
2. God wants us to prosper physically (good health)
3. God wants us to prosper financially

These desires of God were not just meant for the elder to whom John was writing, they were meant for every born again believer. So we must be faithful in reading the Word of God to find His promises; and as we find His promises, we must pray and confess His promises (putting God in remembrance), and when we do so, God brings His Word to pass in our lives.

You are encouraged to not only pray these prayers, but allow God to develop His Word in your life. As you do so, your prayer life will become more exciting. Your prayers will cease from being a chore, and become an exciting part of your life.

As you pray the prayers in this book, you will find that they are personalized for the person praying the prayer. They can, however, be use for any number of people. Simply change the words to apply to your situation.

## For example:

If you needed healing, you might say, "Father, I thank You for Your promise to heal me of all my sickness and diseases, and with the stripes that Jesus Christ bore for my sickness and diseases, I am healed." But if you were praying for someone named John who needed healing, you would say, "Father, I thank You for Your promise to heal John of all his sickness and diseases, and with the stripes that Jesus Christ bore for John's sickness and diseases, I decree that John is healed."

If you have a need for your family, instead of praying "Father, I thank You for supplying all my needs according to Your riches and glory by Christ Jesus, you would simply say, "Father, I thank You for supplying all 'our' needs according to Your riches and glory by Christ Jesus."

Do this with every prayer. The more you use them the more your scripture knowledge will increase, and the more you will be able to pray on your own. As time permits, look up the scriptures that are listed after each prayer. This will enable you to better utilize the scriptures in your own prayers.

Whenever you are reading or studying the bible, keep a notebook handy. Whenever you read a particular scripture that would apply to a specific prayer, write it down and later put it into your own prayer. As you do this more and more, it will help you to remember the scriptures, as well as help you to become better developed in your own personal prayer life.

So again, allow God to bless and teach you, as you use, *The Weapons of Our Warfare.*"


*"So shall my Word be that goeth forth out of my mouth: it shall not return unto me void, but shall accomplish that which I please, and it shall prosper in the thing whereto I sent it."*

*Isaiah 55:11*

# *Chapter I*

# *Daily Prayers and Prayers of Worship and Exaltation*

# *Praise And Worship*

Heavenly Father, as I come before You this day, I enter into Your gates with thanksgiving, and into Your courts with praise. I give You all the thanksgiving, the glory, the honor, and the praise, and I bless Your holy name. For it is a good thing to give thanksgiving and praise to the Lord.

Father, I take this time to magnify, praise, and exalt Your holy name, because You are worthy to be praised; therefore, I will bless You, O Lord, at all times, and Your praise shall continually be in my mouth.

How excellent is Your name in all the earth. There is no one like You, O Lord. For You are far above all nations, kings and kingdoms. You are the God of gods, the King of kings, and the Lord of lords. You are the Alpha and Omega, the First and the Last, the Beginning and the End. Before You, O Lord, there was no other, and You shall outlive eternity itself. You are clothed with beauty, strength, honor, and majesty.

Father, I serve You with gladness, and I come before Your presence with thanksgiving. I know that You, O Lord, are God. For You have made us, and not we ourselves. We are Your people, and the sheep of Your pasture.

You alone do great wonders throughout all the earth. With Your wisdom, You made the heavens; and with the power of Your Word, You stretched out the earth above the waters. You gave us the sun to rule by day, and the moon and stars to rule by night. You are far above all principalities, mights, and dominions; and Your name is far above every name that is named, not only in this world, but also in that which is to come.

Your Kingdom is an everlasting Kingdom. And Your dominion endures throughout all generations. They shall speak of Your glory and talk of Your power forever. Men shall speak of the might of Your terrible acts, and I will declare Your greatness.

I praise You for Your steadfast love that never ceases; for it is renewed every morning. Great is Your faithfulness, O Lord. From the rising of the sun, to the going down of the same, Your name is worthy to be praised.

I have tasted of You, O Lord, and I have found You to be good unto my soul. You are unto my soul as the sweet smell of fragrance, and You are sweeter than the honey in a honeycomb. I bless You, O Lord, from the depths of my soul; and with all that is within me, I bless Your holy name.

In You, O Lord my God, is the greatness, the power, the glory, the victory, and the majesty. For all that is in the heavens and in the earth is Thine. Thine is the Kingdom, O Lord, and You are exalted as head above all. Both riches and honor come from You, and You reign over all. In Your hand is the power to make great, and to give strength unto all.

I love You, O Lord my God. For truly You are my Rock, my Fortress, my Deliverer, my God, and my Strength in whom I will trust. You are my Buckler, the Horn of my Salvation, my High Tower, and the joy and the strength of my life. You are indeed the Shepherd and Bishop of my soul.

I praise You, O Lord my God. I worship You as my Master, my Owner, my King, my Saviour, and my Lord. I offer myself unto You as a living sacrifice. O Lord, let the fruit of my lips give You praise continually, and let the lifting of my hands unto You never cease. Let my prayers be set before You as incense, and let the lifting of my hands unto You be as the evening sacrifice. And Father, as I send forth blessings and praises unto You, let them be as a sweet sound in Your ear.

I love You, O Lord my God; and I pray that You would bless me to exalt You and Your Holy name forever and ever. For You are great, O Lord, and greatly to be praised; and Your greatness is unsearchable and never-ending.

Father, I pray that You would continually bless and

allow me to magnify You, and lift up Your holy, mighty, and majestic name all the days of my life. For Your loving kindness is better than life. Therefore, my lips shall forever praise You, and I will bless You as long as I shall live.

Father, these things I desire and pray above all else: that I will always love You with all of my heart, soul, strength and might; that I may dwell in Your presence all the days of my life; that I may never lose my love for You; that I will always seek You first and foremost all the days of my life, and never stop seeking You, or take my eyes off of You; that You will always be the apple of my eyes; and that You will keep my heart in the love of God, and not allow anything to separate me from You, or take my love from You.

I thank You Father that You are everything to me. For You have revealed Yourself to me through Your Word as *"JEHOVAH,"* the great *"I AM."* For You are everything I need.

When I'm thirsty, You're the Living Water which fills me up until I overflow with gladness. When I'm hungry, You're the Bread of Life which feeds my soul. When I'm in need of a friend, You're a Friend that sticks closer than any brother. When I need a doctor, You're my Great Physician. When I need peace, You're the Prince of Peace. When I'm in battle, You're my Captain in Charge. When I'm in court, You're my Great Advocate. When storms arise, You're my Peace in the midst of every storm, and You become my Bridge over troubled waters.

Father, I pray that Your goodness and mercy follows me this day, as well as throughout all the days of my life, as You bless me to dwell in Your secret place. And I give You all the glory, the honor, the praise, the adoration and thanksgiving.

For Thine is the Kingdom, the Power, and the Glory, forever and ever, AMEN!

## *Scriptures used in this prayer:*

Psalms 100:4
Psalms 92:1
Psalms 18:3
Psalms 34:1
Psalms 8:1
Jeremiah 10:6
Psalms 113:4
Psalms 97:9
Ephesians 1:21
1 Timothy 6:15
Revelation 1:8
Rev 1:11
Psalms 29:2
Psalms 96:6
Job 37:16
Psalms 100:2-3
Psalms 136:4
Ps. 136:5-9
Eph 1:21
Psalms 145:13
Psalms 57:5
Psalms 145:6

Ps 145:11
Lam 3:22-23
Psalms 113:3
Psalms 34:8
Ph 4:18
Psalms 19:10
Ps 103:1-5
1 Chr 29:11-12
Psalms 116:1
2 Sam 22:2-3
Psalms 23:1
Psalms 22:22
Matthew 8:19
1 Cor 6:20
2 Samuel 22:3
John 20:28
Romans 12:1
Ps 63:3-4
Neh 8:6
Psalms 141:2
Hebrews 13:15
1 Chr 16:25

Psalms 145:3
Psalms 63:3-4
Deut 6:5
Psalms 23:6
Romans 8:35
Matthew 6:33
Deut 32:10
Psalms 17:8
Exodus 3:14
John 4:10
John 6:35
Prov 18:24
Mark 2:17
Isaiah 9:6
Joshua 5:13-14
1 John 2:1
Mark 4:39
Psalms 40:2
Psalms 23:6
Psalms 91:1
1 Chr 29:11
Matthew 6:13

# *Daily Prayer*

Father, I come boldly before Your throne of grace thanking and praising You for this day. For this is the day that You have made; therefore, I shall rejoice and be glad in it. I thank You Father that You have given me this day; and I enter into Your gates with thanksgiving, and into Your courts with praise. I give You all the glory and the honor, and I bless Your holy name.

You said that if we acknowledge You in all our ways, You would direct our path. Father, I acknowledge You in all my ways concerning this day, and I thank You for directing my path in every situation. You also said that if we commit our works unto You, that You would establish our thoughts. So I commit all my works unto You now, and I thank You for establishing and directing my every thought throughout this day. I pray that You would be a lamp unto my feet, and a light unto my path today, and guide me with Your eyes and Your Spirit as You order my footsteps.

Father, You said that You desire above all things that we would prosper and be in health, even as we prosper spiritually. I pray first and foremost in my life that You would bless me to prosper spiritually. Bless me to grow in grace and in the knowledge, understanding and usage of Your Word. Bless me to grow in obedience to Your Word – to be a doer of Your Word, and not a hearer only. Bless me to draw close to You, and give me a continuing desire to intimately know You more. For You said that if we draw close to You, then You would draw close to us.

I thank You Father that my soul prospers in You this day, as well as every day. And, as a result, I speak Your Word that I am blessed and prosperous in every area and aspect of my life. I thank You for keeping me in good health and continually healed from the crown of my head to the soles of my feet. I thank You that Your healing virtue flows through me continually. By the authority of Your Word, I confess that no plague, sickness, nor any spirit of infirmity shall come nigh my dwelling, and *"WITH THE STRIPES OF JESUS CHRIST, I AM HEALED, AND I WALK CONTINUALLY IN GOOD HEALTH!"*

Lord, I thank You for being my Shepherd. And as my Shepherd, You said that I would have no need of want, because You promised to supply all my needs according to Your riches in Glory by Christ Jesus. I thank You for Your promise to not only supply all of my needs, but to also supply them exceedingly, abundantly, and above all that I could ask or think. Therefore, I praise and thank You for meeting every need in my life this day and every day of my life – spiritually, physically and financially; and

I thank You also for Your abundant blessings in every area of my life.

I thank You for the hedge of strong and mighty angels which You have set around my family and me, keeping us safe from all hurt, harm, and danger – spiritually, as well as physically. I thank You that they watch over us, protect us, and fight for us.

I thank You Father that no weapon (spiritual or physical) that is formed against me shall prosper in any way, and every tongue that rises against me shall be exposed and condemned. I thank You for rebuking the devourer from every area of my life for my sake. And I pray that Your power and anointing shall be so upon me, that when the enemy comes against me one way, he shall be forced to flee from before me seven different ways.

I thank You that Your Spirit precedes me this day to make all the crooked things straight and the rough areas smooth. I pray therefore, that every trap that the enemy would set out for or against me this day would backfire on him, and work out for my good and for Your glory. For You said that all things work together for good, for those who love the Lord.

I take authority over Satan, every demonic spirit, every principality, and every spirit of wickedness in high places. I bind them from my life this day, and from the lives of my family. I render every demonic spirit against us to be helpless, powerless, ineffective and inoperative to prosper against us or hinder us in any way. Satan, you are under my feet. I pull down every stronghold, and I cast down every wicked and demonic imagination in advance. Satan, I command you by the authority of the name of Jesus Christ that you loose every hold from my life, and to touch not God's anointed.

I thank You Father for giving me the mind of Christ. I pray that Your Spirit would rest, rule, and abide upon me this day with a double portion of Your anointing and power. And I pray that the Glory of the Lord would shine bright from my life this day, as well as every day.

I thank You that the words of my mouth and the meditation of my heart will be acceptable before You this day. I pray that You would set a watch over my mouth, and keep the doors of my lips; and bless me to guard my heart with all diligence, by the discipline of my eyes and the members of my body.

Father, I present myself unto You this day as a living sacrifice. I pray that You would bless me to live my life holy and acceptable unto You, which is my reasonable service. May You keep me from being conformed to the world and the world's way of thinking and living; but rather, help me to be transformed unto Jesus Christ by the renewing of my mind in Your Spirit and Your Word.

I pray that You would help me to walk in the Spirit this day, as well as every day. For You said that if we walk in the Spirit, we shall not fulfill the lust of the flesh. I thank You Father that I walk "not" in the lust of the flesh, but rather, in the power, might, and strength of

Your Spirit. Your Word says that You are able to keep me from falling. Therefore, I trust and depend upon You wholly to sustain me and keep me from falling into sin and mischief. And I pray that You lead me not into temptation, but deliver me from every evil and demonic temptation and snare of the enemy, and help me to walk in the victory that You have given me through Christ Jesus.

Father, I pray that You would give me favor with those who are in authority over me. I pray that as I go upon my job, that those in authority over me will be well pleased with my work. I also thank You for a good working relationship with others whom I work with, as well as those who work under me. I pray that throughout this day, that You would bless me to let my light so shine before those around me, that they will see Your good work (through me), and glorify You, O Lord.

Now Father, I thank You for Your protection, provisions and Your prosperity this day. I thank You also for giving me this day as a day of victory, power and strength. I pray for Your will to be done in my life this day, as Your will is done in heaven. And as I go forth into this day, I rest in confidence knowing, that if You are with me and for me, which I know that You are, then nothing is strong enough to come against me and succeed. I therefore, have a confident and great expectation that You shall take me through this day in victory. So I say, to God be the Glory, for all the things You have done, You are doing, and You shall continue to do in and through my life this day, and all the days of my life. In the name of the Lord, Jesus Christ, I pray, AMEN!

## *Scriptures Used In This Prayer:*

| | |
|---|---|
| *Hebrews 4:16* | *Esther 8:5* |
| *Psalms 118:24* | *Romans 8:28* |
| *Psalms 100:4* | *Matthew 16:19* |
| *Proverbs 3:6* | *Ephesians 6:12* |
| *Proverbs 16:3* | *2 Corinthians 10:4-5* |
| *Psalms 119:105* | *Job 22:28* |
| *Psalms 32:8* | *Isaiah 58:6* |
| *Psalms 37:23* | *1 Chronicles 16:22* |
| *3 John 1:2* | *Romans 12:2* |
| *2 Peter 3:18* | *Isaiah 11:2* |
| *James 1:22* | *2 Corinthians 12:9* |
| *James 4:8* | *2 Kings 2:9* |
| *Philippians 3:10* | *Matthew 5:16* |
| *Psalms 91:10* | *Psalms 19:14* |
| *Isaiah 53:5* | *Psalms 141:3* |
| *Psalms 23:1* | *Proverbs 4:23* |
| *Philippians 4:19* | *Romans 12:1-2* |
| *Ephesians 3:20* | *Jude 1:24* |
| *Psalms 91:11-12* | *Matthew 6:13* |
| *Isaiah 54:17* | *Genesis 39:21* |
| *Malachi 3:11* | *Matthew 6:10* |
| *Deuteronomy 20:4* | *Romans 8:31* |
| *Luke 3:5* | *Jude 1:25* |
| *Psalms 91:3* | |

# *Praying the Names Of God*

Father, I come before Your throne of grace, and I worship You, and thank You for revealing Yourself to us through Your covenant names.

You are *ELELYON*: The Most High God. You are far above all principalities, mights and dominions. Your name is above every name in the heavens and the earth. You are seated in heavenly places with all things under Your feet. And by Your grace, You have made me to be seated with You in heavenly places. And therefore, I also stand on top – with all things under my feet.

You are *ELOHIYM:* The God of creation. You are the creator of the universe, the heavens, the earth, the worlds, and all they that dwell therein. You don't have to find a blessing for me; You are the Great Creator who is able to create a blessing for me.

You are *EL SHADDAI:* You are the God of the "Much More," and You provide more than enough for me. You are the self-sufficient One who supplies all my needs. Because of You, there is no lack in any area of my life. You cause all grace to abound towards me so that I have all sufficiency in all things; and You bless me exceedingly, abundantly and above all I can ask or think.

You are *JEHOVAH:* The Great "I AM." You are the self-existing One who never leads me to what I need, because You are what I need in every situation.

You are *JEHOVAH SHALOM:* The Lord my Peace. You are my Peace that passes all man's understanding. You are my peace in the midst of confusion, trouble, turmoil and chaos; and You are my peace in the midst of every storm in my life.

You are *JEHOVAH NISSI:* The Lord, my Banner. You are my High Tower against the enemy. You are my Shield and Buckler. You are my Victor and my Captain over me, who gives me victory over sin, sickness, poverty and every enemy of my life.

You are *JEHOVAH JIREH:* You are the Lord, my Provider. You are the One who provides for me everything I need according to Your riches in Glory.

You are *JEHOVAH RAPHA:* The Lord that heals me. Because of the stripes of Jesus Christ, no plague, sickness or disease shall come nigh my dwelling. You take sickness and disease away from me, and the number of my days You shall fulfill. And because of You, I am whole, well and sound in my spirit, soul and body.

You are *JEHOVAH T'SIDKENU*: The Lord my righteousness. And because You are my righteousness, You have placed me in right standing with You; and therefore, I can boldly come before Your throne of grace.

You are *JEHOVAH M'KADDESH*: The Lord my sanctification. You have sanctified me, justified me and redeemed me with the blood of the Lamb; and You have made me to be holy – to be used for Your Glory.

You are *JEHOVAH SHAMMAH*: You are always there for me. You will never leave me nor forsake me all the days of my life. You are the same yesterday, today and forever more.

You are *JEHOVAH SABOATH*: The Lord of host. You have assigned strong, mighty and warring angels over my life. You have given them a charge over me to keep me in all my ways. They guard me, protect me, fight for me, and rage in battle for me. And, they carry forth Your Word to bring it to pass in my life.

You are *JEHOVAH ROHI*: The Lord who is my Shepherd, and I shall not want or be in lack of any good or needful thing. You lead me, guide me, and watch over me in all of my ways. And, You are the God who causes goodness and mercy to follow me all the days of my life.

You are *ADONAY*: The Sovereign God. You bought me with a price. Therefore, You are my Master who rules me, my Owner who owns me, and my Lord who directs and controls me.

Now Father I thank You for revealing Yourself to us through Your names. I worship and praise You for Your names, and who You are to me through them. I thank You also for giving us "ONE" name that is a conglomeration of all these covenant names. I also give You praise, adoration and thanksgiving for this one name.

It is a name that is greater and higher than any other name, not only in this world, but also in that which is to come; the name that has and will cause every knee to bow and every tongue to confess that He is Lord; the name that causes demons to tremble and flee at the sound of it; the name that causes yokes and strongholds to be loosed and broken when it is spoken; the only name that brings healing and deliverance; the name that is powerful, awesome, mighty, wonderful, glorious, magnificent and omnipotent – the name of *"JESUS CHRIST!"* AMEN!

# Chapter II

## Prayers for your Family and Marriage

# *For Your*
# *"Young" Children*

Father, in the name of our Lord and Savior, Jesus Christ, I thank You for blessing me with my children, and for entrusting me with them. And I come boldly before You lifting them up, and confessing Your Word concerning my children.

Father, You instructed us to teach and train our children in the ways of the Lord. I therefore ask for Your wisdom on how to teach my children in Your ways and Your Word. I pray that the Word of God which I teach them will be hidden deep within their hearts. And, as a result, when they grow older, they will not error or depart from Your ways or Your Word.

Father, I'm asking that You would help me to live a Godly life before them each day that is holy and acceptable in Your sight. As I do so, I thank You for blessing my children to follow me as I follow You in Your ways, and in obedience to Your Word.

I thank You for the promise of Your Word that You would save us and our household. Therefore, I thank You that my children are saved and covered by the blood of Jesus Christ. I thank You not only for the salvation of their souls, but for the complete salvation of their minds and bodies, as well as their souls.

I confess Your Word over my children that they are obedient and submissive. I confess first of all, that even at a Young age, that my children are obedient and submissive to Your ways and Your Word. I confess secondly, that my children are obedient and submissive to their parents, and the spirit of rebellion is far from them. I thank You that they are receptive and obedient to my/our directions, instructions, guidance and corrections. I confess that my children are respectful to me/us, and they are also respectful to their school and church teachers, as well as other adults in authority in their lives.

I thank You Father that my children have the mind of Christ. I confess that they are not conformed to the world, but they are transformed unto the image of Christ daily. Help them to discern good from bad, right from wrong, and what is Godly from what is evil. Help them to choose the right friends and peers, and not be drawn to do wrong or evil by the wrong crowd. And help them not to be influenced to commit sin and ungodliness by television, movies, music, or other negative influences of the world.

I thank You for the promise of Your Word to keep my children in all their ways. I thank You therefore for keeping them from anything or anyone that would hurt them or do them harm. I thank You and trust You to keep them from drugs, alcohol, smoking, and other substance abuse and addictive habits. Thank You for keeping them from adolescent and premarital sex and sexual experimentation. Thank You for keeping them from child molesters, sexual perverts, and anyone that would attempt to deceive them and exploit their innocence or naiveness.

I thank You for Your strong and mighty angels that You have assigned to watch over my children to protect them, and keep them safe from any and all accidents, hurt, harm and danger. I pray that You would keep them from all shootings, stabbing, and crime or violence of any kind in their schools, as well as any place they may go.

I speak Your Word that my children walk in good health. By the stripes of Jesus Christ I decree that they are healed from the crown of their heads to the soles of their feet of every sickness and disease – and no sickness or disease (adolescent or adult) is able to come near their dwelling.

As my children grow, bless them to increase in knowledge, wisdom, understanding and stature, even as You bless them to increase in the knowledge of Your Word and the fear of the Lord. I speak Your Word that their minds are anointed to remember and retain that which they are taught in school and church, and the things they are taught by me/us. Bless them to be diligent in their schoolwork and in their studies. And as a result, bless them to excel in their grades and in other activities.

I take authority over every demonic spirit, every principality, and every spirit of wickedness in high places. I bind them from my children. I pull down every stronghold and demonic influence from their lives; I cast down every wicked imagination from their minds; I bind and loose every power of witchcraft and sorcery from their minds, hearts and lives. I decree these, and every other demonic and satanic spirit to be off limits to the lives of my children; and I also decree them to be helpless, powerless, inoperative and ineffective against them, by the authority of the name of Jesus Christ.

Now Father, I thank You once again for my children. I commit them unto Your care and unto Your watchful eyes. And as I have committed them unto You, I thank You for blessing them; and I trust in You to keep them in all of their ways, and to bless them with a long, happy, healthy, prosperous, safe, and Godly life.

In the name of Jesus Christ I pray, AMEN!

## *Scriptures Used In This Prayer:*

| | |
|---|---|
| Hebrews 4:16 | Psalms 127:3 |
| Proverbs 22:6 | John 17:15 |
| Psalms 19:14 | 3 John 1:2 |
| Psalms 119:11 | Isaiah 53:5 |
| 2 Thessalonians 3:6-7 | Psalms 91:10 |
| Hebrews 12:14 | Proverbs 9:9 |
| 3 John 1:11 | Luke 2:52 |
| Romans 14:19 | Proverbs 10:7 |
| Acts 11:14 | Matthew 16:19 |
| Ephesians 6:1 | Ephesians 6:12 |
| Colossians 3:20 | 2 Corinthians 10:4-5 |
| Hebrews 13:17 | Job 22:28 |
| Philippians 2:5 | Isaiah 58:6 |
| Romans 12:2 | Psalms 55:22 |
| Hebrews 5:14 | Psalms 37:5 |
| Jude 1:24 | Proverbs 20:7 |
| 2 Timothy 2:22 | Psalms 23:6 |

# *For Your "Adult" Children*

Father, in the name of our Lord and Savior, Jesus Christ, I come before You this day thanking You for my children, and lifting them up before You in prayer.

I thank You for the promise of Your Word to save us and our household, including our children. Therefore I confess Your Word that all of my children are saved. I thank You for their complete salvation of their mind and body, as well as their soul. And I pray that You would cover them afresh and anew each day with Your blanket of love, grace, mercy and forgiveness.

Father, I confess Your Word over my children that they have the mind of Christ, and they are not conformed to the world, but rather, transformed daily into the image of Christ. Father, I confess that my children love You with all of their heart, soul, strength and might; they are obedient to Your Spirit, Your ways and Your Word; and they have a heart and a passion for prayer, Your Word, coming to the House of God, and hearing the Word of God.

I confess Your Word that my children walk "not" under the counsel or the influence of the ungodly, nor do they stand in the way of sinners, nor sit at the seat of the scornful; but their delight is You and in Your Word; and they meditate upon Your Word day and night; and therefore, they have a firm, solid and stable foundation in You like a tree that is planted by the rivers of living waters that shall not be moved. And according to Your Word, I confess that my children are abundantly blessed in every area of their lives, and they are blessed by You to prosper in whatever they do.

I pray that You would help them to walk in obedience to Your Spirit and Your Word. Help them to always choose that which is good over bad, right over wrong, and what is Godly over evil. Help them to choose the right friends and acquaintances. And help them not to be influenced to commit or walk in sin, ungodliness or un-righteousness by any person, group of people, or demonic influence.

I thank You for Your promise to keep my children in all their ways. I thank You for being their Shepherd who protects them at all times from any and all accidents and injuries, and from being victimized in crime, violence or any attack on their lives, intentional or unintentional. I thank You for assigning strong and mighty angels to watch over them and keep them safe from all hurt, harm and danger. And may You also keep them from getting involved in, or addicted to drugs, alcohol, smoking or any other substance abuse or addictive habits.

Lord, may You also be the Shepherd of their provisions. I pray that You would bless them to never be in want, and never be deprived of, or go lack in any good thing. And may You also meet every need in the lives of my children.

I pray that You would divinely lead, guide and direct them by Your Spirit throughout their lives. I pray for Your wisdom and discernment upon them in choosing the right jobs, careers, churches, friends, relationships, and in every venture, opportunity and avenue of their lives.

I speak Your Word that my children walk in good health all the days of their lives. By the stripes of Jesus Christ, I decree that they are continually healed from the crown of their heads to the soles of their feet of every sickness and disease, and no sickness or disease is able to come near their dwelling.

I thank You for the favor of Joseph upon the lives of my children. Father, You gave Joseph favor in every place he went and with every person that was over him. I pray by Your mercy and grace that You would give my children the same spirit of favor upon their lives. Give them favor with every teacher, supervisor and person of authority over them in their schools, upon their jobs, and in every area of their lives, all the days of their lives.

As my children grow, I thank You for blessing them to increase in knowledge, wisdom, understanding and stature, even as You bless them to increase in the knowledge of Your Word and the fear of the Lord.

I take authority over every demonic spirit, every principality, and every spirit of wickedness in high places. I bind them from the lives of my children. I pull down every stronghold and demonic influence from their lives. I cast down every wicked imagination from their minds. I bind and loose every power of witchcraft and sorcery from their minds, hearts and lives. I decree these, and every other demonic and satanic spirit to be off limits to the lives of my children. I also decree them to be helpless, powerless, inoperative and ineffective against my children, by the authority of the name of Jesus Christ.

Father, You told us to cast all our cares and burdens upon You; therefore, I cast all my cares for my children upon You. And as I cast all my cares, worries, and anxieties upon You concerning them, I am persuaded that You will keep my children; for Your Word says that You will keep the things I commit unto You against any evil day (or demonic attack).

Now Father, I thank You once again for my children. I commit them unto Your care and unto Your watchful eyes. I pray that Your goodness and mercy follows my children all the days of their lives; and may You keep them in all of their ways, and bless them with a long, happy, healthy, prosperous, safe, and Godly life.

In the name of Jesus Christ I pray, AMEN!

## *Scriptures Used In This Prayer:*

| | |
|---|---|
| *Hebrews 4:16* | *Ephesians 3:20* |
| *Acts 16:31* | *Psalms 5:8* |
| *Lamentations 3:22-23* | *Psalms 25:5* |
| *Philippians 2:5* | *Psalms 61:2* |
| *Romans 12:2* | *Proverbs 3:6* |
| *Deuteronomy 6:5* | *1 Kings 3:9* |
| *James 1:22* | *3 John 1:2* |
| *Colossians 3:10* | *Isaiah 53:5* |
| *Psalms 1:1-3* | *Psalms 91:10* |
| *1 Peter 1:13-14* | *Genesis 39:21* |
| *Psalms 84:2* | *Genesis 39:2-4* |
| *Hebrews 10:25* | *Genesis 41:38-44* |
| *Galatians 5:16* | *Luke 2:52* |
| *Deuteronomy 30:19* | *Proverbs 1:7* |
| *Galatians 5:1* | *Matthew 16:19* |
| *2 Thessalonians 3:3* | *Ephesians 6:12* |
| *Jude 1:24* | *2 Corinthians 10:4-5* |
| *Psalms 91:11-12* | *Job 22:28* |
| *Psalms 121:7* | *Isaiah 58:6* |
| *Psalms 23:1-2* | *Psalms 55:22* |
| *Deuteronomy 8:9* | *Genesis 2:9* |
| *Philippians 4:19* | *Psalms 37:5* |
| *Psalms 1:3* | *Psalms 23:6* |
| *1 Kings 18:41* | |

# *For Your Husband*

F ather, I come boldly before Your throne of grace in the name of our Lord and Savior, Jesus Christ, lifting up my husband.

You said in Your Word, "a faithful man, who can find?" Father, I confess Your Word that my husband is first of all, a man of God who is faithful unto You, and then faithful unto his wife and his family.

I thank You that my husband is a man of God who loves You with all of his heart, soul, strength and might. I confess that he is a man of God who seeks to know You more and draw near to You. I pray that You would keep his heart – to allow nothing to come between or separate his love from You, or his love from his family.

I confess that my husband is a good provider for his home. I confess that he is a man of God who leads our home in wisdom, love, and the fear of the Lord. I thank You that he is a man of God who seeks Your face daily for divine directions, instructions and guidance concerning his life and his family. I pray that as he seeks Your face, that You would be a lamp unto his feet, a light unto his path, and guide him with Your eyes and Your Spirit, as You order his footsteps for our home and our lives.

I thank You that my husband is a man of God who studies to show himself approved unto You, O God, a workman that need not be ashamed, one who knows how to rightfully divide and skillfully use the Word of truth. I pray that as he studies Your Word, that You would give him revelation knowledge concerning Your Word so that he may teach and instruct his family in the Word and the ways of the Lord.

Father, I thank You for assigning Your ministering angels to be encamped around my husband (continually) to protect him, watch over him, and fight for him. I also thank You for giving them a charge to keep my husband in all his ways – spiritually as well as physically.

I thank You that my husband loves me, even as Jesus Christ loves the church and gave himself for the church. And even as my husband loves me, I thank You that I shall love him and submit myself unto him as unto Christ.

Father, as Your love is renewed for us every morning, I pray that You would bless our love to be renewed for You each day. And, as our love is renewed for You, bless our love, desire and passion to be also renewed and revived for one another each and every day. May there never be a dull moment with my husband, and may the time I spend with him bring joy and excitement to my heart.

As You renew the strength of the eagle, I pray that You would renew his strength. Give him strength in his coming in and his going out – at home, at work, and about. And, by the stripes of Jesus Christ, I confess that he walks continually in good health all the days of his life.

I confess Your Word that my husband is crucified with Christ; nevertheless, he lives; yet it is not him that lives, but Jesus Christ living in him; and the life which he now lives in the flesh, he lives by the faith, power, strength and anointing of the Lord, Jesus Christ.

Father, I pray that You would keep my husband from falling, and present him faultless with exceeding joy. May You keep him from falling to the strange woman, and from falling to the spirit of lust and seduction. I pray that You would lead him away from temptation, and deliver him from every snare and trap of the adversary.

I thank You for the authority You have given us in Christ Jesus; and with that authority, I bind every demonic spirit, every principality, and every spirit of wickedness in high places from my husband's life. I pull down every stronghold in his life, and I cast down every evil and satanic imagination. Satan, I command you to loose every hold from my husband's life, and I render you helpless, powerless, inoperative, and ineffective to operate in his life in any area, or hinder his life in any way, by the authority of the name of Jesus Christ.

I thank You Father that no weapon that is formed against my husband shall be able to prosper, and every tongue that shall rise up against him shall be exposed and ashamed. I thank You for Your promise to rebuke the devourer from his life; and I pray that You would bless my husband with a double portion of Your anointing and power, so that when the enemy comes against him one way, he shall be forced to flee from before him seven different ways.

I thank You Father that my husband has favor with You; therefore, he has favor with man. As he goes upon his job, may You bless him with prosperity and good success. May You bless him in all of his work, and bless him to prosper in everything he does.

Now Father, I commit my husband to You; and I am confident, that according to Your Word, You are able to keep him, sustain him, protect him, and direct him in all his ways, as I have committed him unto You.

In the name of Jesus Christ, I pray, AMEN!

## Scriptures Used In This Prayer:

| | |
|---|---|
| *Hebrews 4:16* | *Isaiah 53:5* |
| *Proverbs 20:6* | *3 John 1:2* |
| *Deuteronomy 4:29* | *Galatians 2:20* |
| *Mark 12:30* | *Jude 1:24* |
| *Philippians 3:10* | *Proverbs 2:16* |
| *James 4:8* | *James 1:14-15* |
| *Romans 8:38-39* | *Matthew 6:13* |
| *Psalms 119:105* | *Matthew 16:19* |
| *Psalms 32:8* | *Ephesians 6:12* |
| *2 Timothy 2:15* | *2 Corinthians 10:4-5* |
| *Psalms 91:11-12* | *1 Samuel 2:26* |
| *Ephesians 5:25* | *Psalms 1:3* |
| *Ephesians 5:22* | *Psalms 37:5* |
| *Lamentations 3:22-23* | *Psalms 55:22* |
| *Psalms 103:5* | |

# *For Your Wife*

F ather, I come boldly before Your throne of grace in the name of our Lord and Savior, Jesus Christ, lifting up my wife.

You said in Your Word, "whoever finds a wife, finds a good thing and obtains favor with You." I thank You Father that You have given me a good thing by blessing me with my wife; and I pray that we find favor with You, through first of all our love for You, and then our love for one another.

I thank You that my wife is a blessing to me in every way. I thank You that she is truly a virtuous woman, her price is far above rubies, and strength and honor are her clothing. I thank You that she does me good and not evil, and she shall continue to do me good all the days of our lives together.

I thank You that she opens her mouth with wisdom, and in her tongue is the law of kindness. I confess that my wife looks well to (takes well care of ) her husband, her children and her household, and does not eat the bread of idleness.

Father, I pray that You would bless me to continually cherish and love my wife as Jesus Christ loves the church, and gave himself for the church. As I love my wife, I thank You that she also loves me and submits herself unto me as unto Christ. I pray that You would bless me to always be pleased with my wife, and bless her to intimately satisfy me at all times, even to the point to where I am ravished with her love.

I thank You Father that my wife is clothed in beauty and charm; and my eyes are drawn only to her, and enticed only by her. I thank You that my heart safely trusts in her and I desire her so, that I have no need, want or desire of spoil from any other woman. I thank You Father that I am not lured or drawn to look upon or lust after the strange woman. I pray that in my wife, are the desires of my heart and my eyes. I thank You that in my eyes, my wife is the most beautiful woman in the entire world, and there is none other as desirous or as beautiful as she.

May You help me to never look upon my wife in a negative way. But as I look upon my wife, may I only see my love for her, and the glory of the Lord upon her all the days of our lives together.

Father, as Your love is renewed for us every morning, I pray that You would bless our love to be renewed for

You each day. And, as our love is renewed for You, bless our love, desire and passion to be also renewed and revived for one another each and every day. May there never be a dull moment with my wife, and may the time I spend with my wife bring joy and excitement to my heart.

As You renew the strength of the eagle, I pray that You would renew my wife's strength. Give her strength in her coming in and her going out – at home, at work, and about.

I thank You Father that my wife seeks You and all of Your righteousness first and foremost in her life; and I pray that You would keep her strong in You, and in the power of Your might. And may You keep her strengthened, established, and settled in You, Your anointing, and Your power. I thank You Father that she is a woman of prayer, who prays effectually and fervently with prayer and supplications, and she studies Your Word to continually show herself approved unto You, O God, a workman that need not be ashamed, knowing how to rightly divide and skillfully use the Word of truth.

I thank You for the authority You have given us in Christ Jesus; and with that authority, I bind every demonic spirit, every principality, and every spirit of wickedness in high places from my wife's life. I pull down every stronghold in her life, and I cast down every evil and satanic imagination. Satan, I command you to loose every hold from my wife's life, and I render you helpless, powerless, inoperative, and ineffective to operate in her life in any area, or hinder her life in any way, by the authority of the name of Jesus Christ.

I thank You Father that no weapon that is formed against my wife will be able to prosper, and every tongue that shall rise up against her shall be exposed and ashamed. I thank You for Your promise to rebuke the devourer from her life; and I pray that You would bless my wife with a double portion of Your anointing and power, so that when the enemy comes against her one way, he shall be forced to flee from before her seven different ways. I pray that You would keep my wife from falling spiritually, as well as physically, and deliver her from every trap and snare of the enemy.

I thank You Father that You have given Your ministering angels a charge to be encamped around my wife (continually) to protect her, watch over her, fight for her, and keep her in all her ways.

I thank You that my wife has favor with You; therefore, she has favor with man. I pray that You would bless her to prosper in everything she does. I pray that as she goes upon on her job, that she will allow the light of Jesus Christ to so shine before the people around her, that they may see her good work, and glorify You, O God.

Now Father, I commit my wife unto You; and I am confident that according to Your Word, You are able to keep her, sustain her, protect her, and direct her in all her ways, as I have committed her unto You.

In the name of Jesus Christ I pray, AMEN!

## *Scriptures Used In This Prayer:*

| | |
|---|---|
| *Hebrews 4:16* | *Colossians 1:23* |
| *Proverbs 18:22* | *Ephesians 6:18* |
| *Proverbs 31:10* | *2 Timothy 2:15* |
| *Proverbs 31:25* | *Matthew 16:19* |
| *Proverbs 31:12* | *Ephesians 6:12* |
| *Proverbs 31:26-27* | *2 Corinthians 10:4-5* |
| *Ephesians 5:25* | *Isaiah 54:17* |
| *Ephesians 5:22* | *Malachi 3:11* |
| *Proverbs 5:19* | *Deuteronomy 28:7* |
| *Proverbs 31:30* | *Jude 1:24* |
| *Proverbs 6:24-27* | *Psalms 91:3* |
| *Song of Songs 6:4* | *Psalms 91:11-12* |
| *Lamentations 3:22-23* | *1 Samuel 2:26* |
| *Psalms 103:5* | *Psalms 1:3* |
| *Isaiah 53:5* | *Matthew 5:16* |
| *Matthew 6:33* | *Psalms 37:5* |
| *Ephesians 6:10* | *Psalms 55:22* |

# *For A Troubled Marriage*

Father, I come boldly before Your throne of grace to find help in this time of trouble in our marriage. For Your Word says that You are a very present help in times of trouble. So I look unto the hills (unto You), from which comes our help. For I know that our help comes only from You.

Father, I know that it is the thief (Satan) who comes to steal, kill, and bring destruction upon our marriage. I recognize that he is the one that desires to steal our happiness and destroy our marriage. So I take authority over Satan, and over every principality, every demonic spirit, and every spiritual wickedness in high places, and I bind them from our marriage, by the authority of the name of Jesus Christ!

Father, You said that what You have joined together, that we should allow no man, nor any demon in hell to put asunder or separate. Father, I believe that You put us together; so I refuse to let the devil take hold and destroy our marriage. I cast down every spirit of arguing, fussing, fighting, discord and division. I render these, as well as every other demonic attack against our marriage to be helpless, powerless, inoperative and ineffective against us.

I thank You Father that the weapons of our warfare are not carnal, but mighty through God, to the pulling down of strongholds, and casting down imaginations. Therefore, I pull down every stronghold of Satan in our marriage; I cast down every wicked and demonic thought, imagination and influence that is upon or against our marriage. I enter into the strong man's house (Satan) with one who is stronger than he, (the Lord, Jesus Christ), and I take back what rightfully belong to us. I take back our peace, harmony, love, affection, and everything else that God has given and promised us for our marriage. Satan, I decree that you are defeated in our marriage, and you are under our feet. I decree all these things by the powerful, magnificent and invincible name of the Lord, Jesus Christ.

Father, I also thank You for the power and authority that You have given to us to speak to our circumstances and command them to be removed; therefore, I speak to this mountain of troubles in our marriage, and I command them to be removed, uprooted, and cast into the sea. And even as Jesus spoke, and calmed the raging sea with the power of His Word, I also speak the Word of the Living God to this sea of troubles in our marriage, and I command them to be at *"Peace, and be still!"*

I thank You Father that this satanic weapon that has been formed against us shall "not" prosper, and every tongue that shall rise against us shall be exposed and brought to an open shame. I thank You for contending with the enemy as he contends with us through this attack; and may You fight on our behalf, and rebuke the devourer from our marriage, for our sake.

Father, You said that You would perfect that which concerns us; and You know these troubles concern us. So I pray that You would perfect our marriage from these troubles, and bless our marriage to mature in Christ.

Lord, You are our Shepherd, and as our Shepherd, I pray that You would help us not to follow the voice of the stranger (Satan), but help us to follow Your voice (our Great Shepherd). Therefore, I cast down every thought and imagination of separation, infidelity, unfaithfulness, and divorce; and I thank You that neither my spouse nor I shall listen to the voice of Satan.

Father, You said that the effectual, fervent prayers of a righteous man avail much. I know that I am not righteous of my own works, but I am made righteous through Jesus Christ. Therefore, I thank You that my prayers for our marriage avail much in victory.

I pray that You would bless our love to grow stronger and stronger, first of all for You, and then for one another. And as our love grows, give us a desire to please each other more and more. I pray that as we find faults and shortcomings in each other, that You would help us to be patient with one another, and bless our love to over-come our faults and differences. For Your Word says that love covers a multitude of faults.

Father, You instructed us to always remember our first love. So I pray that You would bless us to remember how it was when we first met. May You restore and revive that same first love affection and desire within our hearts, and help us to keep our love continually stirred passionately for one another.

I pray that You would help us not to become con-formed to what Satan would have us to see in each other, but bless us to rather, become transformed and renewed daily to see what You would have us to see in each other. May You renew our minds so that we see each other as exciting, attractive, sensuous, and more desirable than ever before. Bless us to care about what pleases each other, help us to become more sensitive to each other's needs and desires, and help us not to be selfish, but rather giving to one another.

I pray that You would help us to walk in unity, and in the spirit of agreement. And help us to both speak the same things (in the spirit of unity) and be on one accord in Christ.

I thank You for the peace of God in our marriage – the peace that passes all understanding. May You keep us in Your perfect peace (rather than confusion and conten-tion), and help us to keep our eyes and our minds stayed upon on You.

Now Father, I thank You for Your Word, and how that Your Word does not return unto You void, but it accomplishes that in which You send it to perform. So as I have prayed Your Word through this prayer, I thank You for our victory, and for our deliverance, restoration and reconciliation. I give You all the glory, the honor and the praise for what You have already done (by faith), and for what You shall continue to do in our marriage.

In the name of Jesus Christ, I pray. AMEN!

## Scriptures Used In This Prayer:

| | |
|---|---|
| *Hebrews 4:16* | *Psalms 138:8* |
| *Psalms 46:1* | *Psalms 23:1* |
| *Psalms 121:2* | *John 10:27* |
| *John 10:10* | *John 10:2* |
| *Luke 10:19* | *John 10:3-5* |
| *Luke 9:1* | *2 Corinthians 10:5* |
| *Matthew 19:6* | *James 5:16* |
| *Hebrews 11:24* | *1 Peter 4:8* |
| *Matthew 16:19* | *Revelation 2:4* |
| *Ephesians 6:12* | *Ephesians 5:25* |
| *2 Corinthians 10:4-5* | *Ephesians 5:22* |
| *Job 22:28* | *Romans 12:2* |
| *Isaiah 58:6* | *Psalms 103:5* |
| *Matthew 12:29* | *2 Corinthians 4:16* |
| *Matthew 21:21* | *Ephesians 4:23* |
| *Mark 4:39* | *1 Corinthians 1:10* |
| *Isaiah 54:17* | *Philippians 4:7* |
| *Isaiah 49:25* | *Isaiah 55:11* |
| *Exodus 14:14* | *1 John 5:4* |
| *Malachi 3:11* | |

# Chapter III

## Prayers For Safety, Protection and Rest

# *A Prayer Of The 91st Psalm*

## *A Prayer of God's Protection, Deliverance and Safety*

I thank You Father, O Most High God, for blessing me to dwell in Your secret place, under the shadow of Your wings of protection, in true intimacy with You, embraced and sheltered by Your power and Your precious love.

I confess and say unto You, O Lord, that You alone are my refuge, my fortress, and my place of protection from dangers and distress. You are also my stronghold and my defense against my enemies. You are the only God in whom I serve. And only in You will I confidently place my trust.

I trust not in my own abilities, nor in my own wisdom or strength; but I trust in You, O Lord, to deliver me from the snares, traps and the deceptive and sinful temptations and entanglements of Satan. You are also my deliverer from every sickness, disease and pestilence.

I thank You Father for covering me with Your feathers of safety, warmth and love – far out of the reach and grasp of my enemies. And the truth and power of Your Word is my defense, my shield and my protection around me.

Because I dwell in Your secret place, I shall not be afraid of the spiritual dangers or demonic tactics and attacks of Satan; nor shall I be afraid of the plots of the wicked (people) that he would influence and use to fight against me.

Neither shall I worry, fret nor be afraid of unseen and unknown catastrophic disasters or deadly diseases; nor of sudden death or destruction of my life, or destruction of Your blessings in my life.

Even though many fall to the temptations and destruction of the enemy on one side, and tens of thousands suffer lack and are afflicted with sickness, disease and other calamities on the other side, none of these evils shall fall upon or come near me.

I will see with my eyes the punishable rewards and destruction of the wicked and the unjust, but I shall not partake in their sufferings.

Because I have made You, O Lord, the Most High God, my abode, my dwelling place and my habitation, no evil shall be able to fall upon or touch me, and no sickness or disease can come upon me, or even come near my home or my family.

I thank You Father for commanding Your angels to watch over me, and protect me wherever I go. They are encamped in a hedge of protection around me. They shall preserve me, defend me, and keep me safe from all hurt, harm and danger.

I thank You for giving me power and authority in Christ Jesus over every demon and devil. And, because I am hid in Christ in heavenly places, even as Christ has all things under His feet, I also have all things under my feet. And therefore, even the demonic and satanic principalities, powers and wicked spirits in high places are trampled under my feet.

Because I have set my heart upon You, to love You and serve You with all of my heart, my soul, my strength and my might; And, because I reverence You, and worship Your holy, mighty, majestic, precious and glorious name, You shall deliver me from every attack of the enemy, and none of his weapons shall prosper against me.

Because I make my habitation and dwelling place in You, O Lord, whenever I am in trouble of any kind, and I need to call upon You for my help, You will be right there as always to answer me, and honor me with Your mighty hand of deliverance:

And, You will show me the salvation of the Lord by blessing me with a long, healthy, safe and prosperous life, and give unto me Your many wondrous blessings.

## *Scriptures Used In This Prayer:*

*Psalms, Chapter 91*

# *For Safety (General)*

Father, I come boldly before Your throne of grace asking for Your divine safety and protection over _____.

Father, in Your Word You instructed us to always pray, and "not faint" in our praying, so that we will not fall into dangers, trials and temptations. Therefore, I pray Your Word over _____, that You would keep ____ sheltered, in Your arms of safety.

I commit _____ into Your hands concerning this (*day, time period or occasion*). For You told us in Your Word that You are able to keep, take care of, and bring to pass the things that we commit unto You in prayer.

I pray that You would assign strong and mighty angels to watch over _____. May You encamp them in a hedge of protection around _____ to keep _____ in all ___ ways. I thank You that Your angels continually bear _____ up in their hands, so that _____ will not fall into any affliction in any way.

I thank You that Your mighty angels fight for _____, guard ____, protect _____, and watch over _____ to keep _____ from all accidents, hurt, harm and dangers.

Father, I thank You for the power and authority that You have given us over the devil and over every evil and demonic spirit; and with that authority, I bind Satan, every principality, and every spirit of wickedness from hurting or harming _____ in any way, by the authority of the name of Jesus Christ.

I confess Your Word that no weapon that is formed against _____ shall be able to prosper against _____ in any way. I pray that You would anoint _____ with a double portion of Your anointing; whereas, when the enemy comes against _____ one way, he shall be forced to flee seven different ways; for You promised to rebuke the devourer for our sake.

Father, in Your Word, You promised us long life. And I am fully persuaded that You shall fulfill Your promise, as You continually show ____ Your salvation, and bless _____ with a long, safe, healthy and prosperous life.

Father, You instructed us to cast our cares and our worries upon You, and You would sustain us. Therefore, I cast my cares and worries concerning _____ upon You; and I am confident, that according Your Word, You shall sustain _____, and bring ____ to a safe and expected end. For Your Word says that You are faithful to keep us from all evil.

Because I have put my trust in You to watch over _____, I thank You for allowing Your peace to rest upon me concerning _____. And may You keep me from worry, anxieties and fear concerning _____ and _____ safety.

As I have committed _____ unto Your care, I rest in the confidence of Your Word, knowing that if You are with and for _____, which I know that You are, then nothing is strong enough or able to come against _____ and succeed.

Now Father, I thank You and praise You for victory in Christ Jesus in all things concerning _____, and for _____ complete salvation and safety.

In the name Jesus Christ, I pray, AMEN!

## Scriptures Used In This Prayer:

| | |
|---|---|
| *Hebrews 4:16* | *Malachi 3:11* |
| *Matthew 26:41* | *Psalms 91:16* |
| *Psalms 37:5* | *Psalms 55:22* |
| *Jeremiah 1:12* | *Jeremiah 29:11* |
| *Psalms 91:10-12* | *2 Thessalonians 3:3* |
| *Matthew 16:19* | *John 14:1* |
| *Isaiah 54:17* | *Philippians 4:7* |
| *Deuteronomy 28:7* | *Romans 8:31* |

# *For Safety When Traveling By Car*

Father, I come boldly before Your throne of grace asking for Your hand of safety and protection as I take this trip.

I ask that as I go on this trip, that Your angels would be encamped round about me and my car, keeping me safe from all accidents, hurt, harm and danger.

I pray that You would not only keep me from running into others on the road, but I pray that You would also keep others driving on the road from running into me.

Father, I pray that as I drive, may You keep me awake and fully alert at all times. I bind the spirit of slumber from my eyes and from my mind while I am driving. Instead, I bind unto me the spirit of alertness, as well as soundness in my thinking and judgment.

Father, I pray that You would keep the car fully operational and functional. May You keep the car from having any mechanical breakdowns, failures or malfunctions; and may You bless every part of this car to operate and perform in perfection throughout this trip.

I bind every demonic spirit of Satan that would attempt to come against me on this trip. And I render every spirit of Satan helpless, powerless, inoperative and ineffective to stop or hinder this trip, or to cause any accidents of any kind, by the authority of the name of Jesus Christ.

Now, Father, I commit this trip to You and unto Your care. And, I commit my safety and protection unto Your hands. For I am fully persuaded in Your Word that You shall keep me in Your care and protection, and take me to my destination in Your arms of safety.

In the name of Jesus Christ, I pray, AMEN!

## *Scriptures Used In This Prayer:*

*Hebrews 4:16*
*Psalms 91:11-12*
*Psalms 91:1-13*
*Psalms 121:3*
*Psalms 132:4*
*Proverbs 6:4*
*2 Timothy 1:7*
*Matthew 16:19*
*Psalms 37:5*
*Romans 4:21*

# *For Safety When Traveling By Plane*

Father, I come boldly before Your throne of grace asking for Your hand of safety and protection as I prepare to take this flight.

Father, I pray that as I take this flight, that Your angels would be encamped round about this plane keeping me, as well as all the passengers aboard this plane safe from all hurt, harm and danger.

I pray for the pilots of this plane – that You would help them to fly and operate this plane with knowledge, skill, wisdom and alertness in all they do. I pray that You would also bless them to operate this plane in complete soberness and soundness in their judgment and thinking.

Father, I pray that You would keep this plane fully operational and functional. May You keep it from having any mechanical failures, breakdowns or malfunctions. And, may You bless every part of this plane to operate and perform in perfection throughout this flight.

Father, Your Word says that You make the crooked things straight and the rough areas smooth. I pray therefore, that You would give this plane a smooth takeoff and landing. And may You bless this flight to also be a smooth and calm flight without turbulence.

I bind the spirit of fear from my heart and mind; for You have not given me a spirit of fear, but a spirit of power, and of love, and the sound mind of Christ. So, as I fly, help me to rest with Your peace upon my heart and my mind the entire flight.

I bind every demonic spirit of Satan that would attempt to come against me on this trip. And I render every spirit of Satan to be helpless, powerless, inoperative and ineffective to cause any accidents or problems with this flight, by the authority of the name of Jesus Christ.

Now Father, I pray this prayer over this flight and all of my connecting flights. I commit them unto You and Your care. And, I commit my safety and protection unto Your hands. For I am fully persuaded in Your Word that You shall keep me in Your care and protection, and take me to my destination in Your arms of safety. In the name of Jesus Christ, I pray, AMEN!

## *Scriptures Used In This Prayer:*

| | |
|---|---|
| *Hebrews 4:16* | *Isaiah 26:3* |
| *Psalms 91:11-12* | *Matthew 16:19* |
| *1 Thessalonians 5:6* | *Psalms 37:5* |
| *2 Timothy 1:7* | *Romans 4:21* |
| *Luke 3:5* | *Luke 15:27* |

# *When You Are Fearful Or Afraid*

Father, I come boldly before Your throne of grace to find encouragement and help in a time of need from fear.

Father, because You are my Light, my Salvation, and the strength of my life, I have no need to fear or be afraid. When the wicked come against me, they shall stumble and fall. And though a host of my enemies (of demon spirits) encamp against me, my heart shall not fear; for I shall be confident in You and Your strength to protect me.

I thank You Father that You have not given me a spirit of fear, but a spirit of power, and of love, and of a sound mind. When I walk through the valleys and the shadows of death, which are the dangers around me, I shall fear no evil; for You, O Lord, are with me; and Your rod and Your staff shall comfort me.

I thank You Father for blessing and allowing me to dwell in the secret place of the Most High, and abide under Your Almighty shadow of protection. And I say of

You, O Lord, that You are my Refuge and my Fortress. You are my God, in whom I will trust to protect and keep me.

According to Your Word, O Lord, You promised to deliver me from every snare and danger which should come against me. You also promised to cover me with Your feathers of comfort, and keep me under Your wings of protection.

I thank You for assigning strong and mighty angels to watch over me. I thank You for encamping them in a hedge of protection around me to fight for me, guard me, protect me, keep me in all my ways, and deliver me from all accidents, hurt, harm, dangers and afflictions.

I thank You for the power and the authority You have given me over the devil and over every evil and demonic spirit; and with that authority, I bind every principality and every spirit of wickedness from my life; and by the authority of the name of Jesus Christ, I render them helpless, powerless, inoperative and ineffective against me or my surroundings in any way.

I thank You Father that the weapons of our warfare are not carnal, but mighty through God, to the pulling down of strongholds and casting down imaginations; and by the authority of the name of Jesus Christ, I pull down every stronghold of fear, doubt, worry and unbelief, both now and henceforth; and I refuse to be entangled any further with the bondage of fear.

I thank You for contending with every physical person and every demonic spirit that would come against or contend with me. I thank You for fighting on my behalf, and for being my strong tower and my defense against the attacks of the enemy.

I thank You that no weapon that is formed against me shall be able to prosper, and every tongue that shall rise against me shall be condemned. I thank You for disabling and disarming every weapon that is formed against me (physical and spiritual). I decree that every weapon that the enemy launch against me will backfire on him, and work for my good and Your glory. For You said that all things work together for good, for those who love You.

Father, I set my love upon You; and I thank You for filling me with Your love, and encompassing Your love around me. For Your Word says that perfect love (the love of God) will cast out all fear.

I thank You for keeping me in Your peace in this, and every situation – the peace that passes all understanding. And I pray that You would help me to keep my heart and mind continually stayed upon You.

Now Father, I thank You for my deliverance from fear. And I rest in this confidence: knowing that if You are for me and with me, which I know that You are, then nothing is strong enough or able to come against me and succeed. So Father, I praise You for my complete salvation and safety, and for Your divine peace upon my heart, mind and spirit.

In the name of Jesus Christ I pray, AMEN!

## *Scriptures Used In This Prayer:*

*Hebrews 4:16*
*Psalms 27:1-5*
*2 Timothy 1:7*
*Psalms 23:4*
*Psalms 91:1-16*
*Luke 9:1*
*Matthew 16:19*
*Ephesians 6:12*
*2 Corinthians 10:4-5*
*Job 22:28*
*Isaiah 58:6*
*Isaiah 49:25*
*Psalms 16:8*
*Deuteronomy 1:30*
*Psalms 61:3*
*Proverbs 18:10*
*Isaiah 54:17*
*Romans 8:28*
*Psalms 91:14*
*Psalms 32:7*
*1 John 4:18*
*Isaiah 26:3*
*Philippians 4:7*
*Psalms 91:15*
*Romans 8:31*
*1 John 5:4*

# *A Prayer At Bedtime For Safe, Restful and Sound Sleep*

Father, I come before Your throne of grace giving You thanksgiving and praise for this day, and thanking You for Your provisions for my life this day.

I thank You for keeping me safe throughout this day from all hurt, harm and danger, and for blessing me with Your wisdom, instructions and Your guidance.

I thank You also for walking with me throughout this day, and for providing me with Your help and strength. Because, it was only by Your help and strength that I made it through this day. So Father, for these, and all of Your loving kindness and many wonderful blessings, I give You all the praise, honor, glory, adoration and thanksgiving for this day.

Now, Father, as I prepare to lie down to sleep, I ask for Your continued hand of grace to be upon me. Your Word says that You give to Your beloved, *"sweet sleep."* So therefore, I ask according to Your Word for sweet, sound, restful and peaceful sleep tonight. And, even as You sanctify our souls with the blood of Jesus Christ, I'm asking that You would also sanctify and purify my sleep and my dreams with Your Spirit.

Father, You instructed us to meditate upon Your Word through the day and also through the night. So as I would put Your Word upon my mind, may Your Word saturate my mind, my heart, and my conscious, as well as my entire subconscious being – giving no place to the devil.

If I have committed any sins or transgressions today (knowing or unknowingly), I repent of them now. I ask that You would forgive me of them, and have mercy upon me according to Your loving kindness, and according to the multitude of Your tender mercy. And I pray that You would blot out all of my transgression, sins, iniquities and wrong doings with the blood of the Lord, Jesus Christ.

Father, I thank You for the authority You have given us in Christ Jesus; and with that authority, I bind each and every satanic spirit from my mind, my sleep and my dreams. And I decree by my authority in Christ Jesus that my mind, my sleep and my dreams are closed and off limits to every demon and demonic influence and intervention.

Father, I commit this night's sleep unto You. As I lie down to sleep, I commit my life and my soul unto Your hands to watch and take me through the unconscious toils of the night. And I trust in You that even as You have guided and taken me through this day, that You will also safely guide and take me through this night.

Now Father, as You take me through this night and wake me up in the morning, I pray that You would wake me up well refreshed in my mind and my body. May You awaken me renewed in my spirit, with the joy and peace of God upon me. And, may You also awaken me with a song of praise upon my mind and my heart, ready and willing to worship You and fellowship with You in this new day to come.

In the name of Jesus Christ, I pray, AMEN!

## *Scriptures Used In This Prayer:*

| | |
|---|---|
| *Hebrews 4:16* | *James 5:15* |
| *Philippians 4:19* | *1 John 1:9* |
| *Psalms 23:4* | *Psalms 51:1* |
| *Psalms 27:1* | *Matthew 16:19* |
| *Matthew 6:13* | *Job 22:28* |
| *Psalms 127:2* | *Psalms 37:5* |
| *Proverbs 3:24* | *Proverbs 3:5* |
| *Psalms 4:8* | *Psalms 31:3* |
| *Matthew 11:29* | *Ephesians 4:23* |
| *Philippians 4:7* | *Jeremiah 31:26* |
| *James 4:8* | *Nehemiah 8:10* |
| *1 Thessalonians 5:23* | *Philippians 4:7* |
| *Psalms 1:2* | *Psalms 40:3* |
| *Ephesians 4:27* | *Psalms 34:1* |

# Chapter IV

# Prayers for Healing and Physical Strength

# *For Healing*

Father, I come boldly before Your throne of grace to obtain help in a time of need for healing and restoration in my body. For You said that You desire above all things that we would prosper and be in health.

Father, You instructed us not to forget the benefits that You have given to us as children of God. For You said that You would forgive us of our sins and iniquities, and You would heal us of all our sickness and diseases. Therefore, as a child of the Most High God, and by faith in Your Word, I receive my benefit of healing in my body.

I thank You for being the God who heals me from all of my sickness and diseases; for You are the One who take sickness and disease from me; and You promised to fulfill the number of my days. I thank You now, Father, for fulfilling the promise of Your Word to take this infirmity from my body.

Father, even as You have saved me, and You have begun a good work in my life, I am confident that You will perform and complete it; for Your Word tells us that with long life You will satisfy us and show us Your salvation. So I thank You Father for healing me of this infirmity, and blessing me with a long and healthy life.

Father, I stand upon, and confidently speak Your Word over my body, that the Lord Jesus Christ was wounded for my transgressions, He was bruised for my iniquities, the chastisement of my peace was upon Him, and *"WITH HIS STRIPES, I AM HEALED!"*

I speak Your Word that this weapon of sickness that has been formed against my body shall no longer prosper. For Your Word says that You will contend with the enemy that contends with me. So as this enemy of sickness contends with me through this physical attack upon my body, I thank You for contending with this sickness, fighting on my behalf, and rebuking this spirit from me. For You also promised me that You would rebuke the devourer for my sake.

Father, You said that it's the thief (the devil), who comes to steal, kill, and destroy; but You said that You came to give us life, and life more abundantly. So as the enemy has tried to afflict my body, I enter into the strong man's house (Satan), with One who is even stronger than he (the Lord Jesus Christ), and I take back my health and strength which rightfully belongs to me; because Father, You told us in Your Word, that healing is the children's (of God) bread. It belongs to us!

Father, I thank You that You have made us kings and priests unto the Most High King, Jesus Christ; and You said that when a king shall decree a thing, it shall be established. So I decree and declare, by the authority of Your Word, that I am healed totally, completely and continually from the crown of my head to the soles of my feet, and I walk in good health!

I thank You for giving us authority to speak to our circumstances. Therefore, by Your authority in the name of Jesus Christ, I speak unto my mountain of infirmity before me, and I command it to be removed, uprooted, and cast into the sea. And even as Jesus spoke to the fig tree and told it to die, and it died, I speak to this sickness, and I command it to die at the very root, and not spring up again; because Father, You told us in Your Word that affliction shall not rise upon us the second time.

I bind and loose every spirit of sickness and disease that has been launched against my body. I also pull down every stronghold spirit of infirmity that has attacked my body. I render these, as well as every other satanic and demonic spirit to be helpless, powerless, inoperative and ineffective against my body, by the authority of the name of Jesus Christ. For greater is He (Jesus Christ) that is in me (who gives me power over sickness and disease), than the enemy (of Satan through this sickness) that is in the world.

As King Ahasuerus gave Esther the authority to reverse the demonic plot against the people of God by Haman, by the authority of a much higher king – One who is King of all kings and Lord of all lords, King Jesus Christ, I reverse this demonic plot and curse of sickness and disease against my body. And I command every spirit of infirmity to cease its work against my body, and return back from which it came.

By the authority of the name of Jesus Christ, I command every cell, every molecule, every organ, and every part of my body to fall in line, and operate and perform in perfection, the way that God created and made them to work and perform.

Father, Your Word says to *"let the redeemed of the Lord say so."* I thank You for redeeming me by the blood of the Lamb, Jesus Christ. So, by the authority of Your Word, I *"say so"* that I am healed of this affliction, and I walk in good health.

Now Father, I thank You that my prayers avail much in victory. For You said, *"the effectual fervent prayer of a righteous man availeth much."* Father, as I have prayed this prayer, I thank You that Your Word does not return unto You void, but it shall accomplish that which You send it to perform. I therefore release my faith by the Word of God which I have prayed. And again, I confess, ***"WITH THE STRIPES OF JESUS CHRIST, I AM HEALED!"***

In the name of Jesus Christ, I pray, and I receive my healing, AMEN!

## *Scriptures Used In This Prayer:*

*Hebrews 4:16*
*3 John 1:2*
*Psalms 103:2-5*
*Exodus 15:26*
*Exodus 23:25*
*Exodus 23:26*
*Philippians 1:6*
*Psalms 91:16*
*Isaiah 53:5*
*Isaiah 54:17*
*Isaiah 49:25*
*Malachi 3:11*
*John 10:10*
*Matthew 12:29*
*Matthew 15:22-28*

*Revelation 1:6*
*Job 22:28*
*Matthew 21:21*
*Matthew 21:19-20*
*Nahum 1:9*
*Matthew 16:19*
*Ephesians 6:12*
*2 Corinthians 10:4-5*
*Isaiah 58:6*
*Esther 8:5*
*1 Timothy 6:15*
*James 5:16*
*Isaiah 55:11*
*Isaiah 53:5*

# *When You Need "Physical" Strength To Keep Going*

Father, in the name of the Lord, Jesus Christ, I come boldly before You asking for Your help in the form of physical strengthening in my body.

Your Word says that we can look unto You for help and strength. So I look unto You and ask this day for Your help and strength in my body. Because even though I am tired in my body, I must go on. So by faith in Your Word, I receive Your divine strength.

Father, You said in Your Word that as we wait upon You, that You would renew our strength. So as I continue to wait upon You, by serving You with gladness, praise and thanksgiving, I thank You for blessing me with inner strength. And as You renew the strength of eagles, I thank You for also blessing me to mount up with the wings of Your (renewed) strength in my mind and my body.

Father, I thank You for empowering me, reviving me, and rejuvenating me with renewed strength to run (in my work and obligations) and not become weary in my body or my mind. I thank You for also empowering me to continue to walk by the faith, power, strength and the anointing of Your Word, and not faint in my walk with You.

As You renew my strength in the natural, I thank You for also renewing my spiritual strength. May You renew my faith in You, my desire for You, and my hunger for You and Your Word. And may You keep me steadfast, unmovable, and abounding in You in my spirit and my soul, as well as my body.

I thank You for the promise of Your Word to be as a well of living water within us. So Father, I draw from this well, the physical strength, stamina and endurance I need.

Father, I thank You for the power and the authority that You have given to us to speak to our circumstances and situations. For You said, let the weak confess that he is strong. So by the power and the authority of Your Word, I speak Your Word unto my body and I decree that *"I AM STRONG IN YOU, O LORD, AND IN THE POWER OF YOUR MIGHT!"*

Father, even as You supernaturally anointed Samson with physical strength (in his body) from above, I pray that You would also anoint me with supernatural strength in my body to continue to go forth in the power and might of Your strength to accomplish my work, jobs and tasks that are before me.

I thank You for redeeming the time for me when I sleep. When I lie down to sleep, I pray that You would anoint me with deep, sound and restful sleep. And, when I awaken (no matter how short the time of sleep), I thank You for blessing me to awaken completely refreshed and renewed in my body.

Now Father, I thank You for being my Great Shepherd who restores my soul and my strength. And as I have prayed Your Word, I thank You for the manifestation of Your Word to give unto me restoration, regeneration, strength and endurance in my body.

In the name of Jesus Christ, I pray, AMEN!

## *Scriptures Used In This Prayer:*

*Hebrews 4:16*              *Galatians 6:9*
*Psalms 121:1-2*           *Lamentations 3:23*
*Isaiah 40:31*             *1 Corinthians 15:58*
*Psalms 100:2*             *John 4:14*
*Psalms 100:4*             *Joel 3:10*
*Hebrews 13:15*            *Judges 14:5-6*
*Exodus 15:2*              *Psalms 127:2*
*2 Samuel 22:4*            *Psalms 103:5*
*Psalms 111:1*             *Ephesians 4:23*
*Psalms 103:1-5*           *Psalms 23:3*
*Isaiah 40:31*

# Chapter V

# Prayers for Finances, Prosperity and Needs

# *Blessings And Prosperity*

F ather, I come boldly before Your throne of grace, thanking and praising You for Your blessings and prosperity upon my life, and upon the lives of my family. According to Your Word, You said that You desire above all things that I may prosper and be in health, even as my soul prospers; therefore, I know that it is Your will for me to prosper.

Father, I thank You first of all, that my soul prospers in You. I thank You that I prosper daily in the knowledge and understanding of Your Word, and that I become rooted, grounded, settled, and established in Christ Jesus.

I thank You that according to Your Word, You have established us as kings and priests unto the Most High King, Jesus Christ. Father, You said in Your Word, *"when a king shall decree a thing, it shall be established."* Therefore, I decree and declare according to Your Word, that I am blessed in the city and blessed in the field; I am above only and not beneath; I am the head and not the tail; I am blessed coming in and blessed going out; I am the lender and not the borrower. I thank You that I am blessed upon my job, and blessed in my home. I confess also that my family is blessed, and my children are blessed and prosperous all the days of their lives.

I thank You Father that I am blessed in my mind with a sound mind, and with the peace of God that passes all understanding. I thank You for blessing me in my body with good health. I thank You for making me to lie down in green pastures, which are the abundance of Your blessings; and Your blessings are continually upon me and overtaking me in every area. I thank You that the windows of heaven are open for me, and You are constantly pouring me out the abundance of Your blessings upon my life – spiritually, physically and financially, whereby I do not have room enough to contain them.

I thank You Father that You have made known Your thoughts towards us – thoughts of good things and blessings for us and not of evil. You instructed us to say continually that You are magnified and You take pleasure in prospering us. So I confess according to Your Word, both now and continually, that *"YOU ARE MAGNIFIED O LORD, AND YOU TAKE PLEASURE IN PROSPERING ME"* in every area of my life.

I thank You for opening doors of prosperity and success for me that no man can shut. I thank You for also closing every door of failure and defeat in my life, which no man can open. And I pray that You would anoint the works of my hands, whereby I may prosper in everything I do.

Father, I pray that You would bless me to keep my eyes upon You continually. Help me to seek You and Your will, first and foremost in my life. For You said in Your Word, that if I seek first the Kingdom of God and all of Your righteousness, You would bless the desires of my heart to be added unto me, and bless me to prosper in everything I do. I thank You therefore that I am blessed and prosperous in my spiritual life, my marriage (if married), my job, and my finances. And Father, I pray that Your goodness and mercy follows me all the days of my life, in every area of my life.

Father, You promised in Your Word that if I would walk in Your ways, that You would bless me to prosper, and You would cause my leaves not to wither. Therefore, I confess Your word that the leaves of my health shall not wither, and the leaves of my finances shall not wither. I also confess that the leaves of my car, my home and my household appliances and other household equipment and furnishings shall not wither. I decree that God's blessings are upon them to last, and Satan cannot bring destruction on God's blessing in my life in any area or in any way. I decree this by the authority of the Word of the Living God in the name of Jesus Christ.

I take authority over every hindering spirit of the enemy. I bind them from my life, and I render them helpless, powerless, inoperative, and ineffective to hinder my life in any way, by the authority of the name of Jesus Christ. I pull down every stronghold of the enemy, and I cast down every wicked spirit that Satan would attempt to use against me.

Father, according to Your Word, if an enemy is caught stealing, he must return seven-fold of that which he has stolen. Father, I have caught the enemy. For Your Word has revealed and exposed Satan as the thief, who comes to steal, kill, and destroy. So Satan, by the authority of the name of Jesus Christ, I command you to return seven-fold of everything you have stolen from every area of my life.

Father, I thank You that this is a prosperous day, week, month, and year for me, and the doors of success have been opened. I confess that I shall succeed in everything in Christ, because every door of failure has been closed, and I shall not know defeat. And I am fully persuaded, that what You have promised in Your Word, You are well able to perform in my life.

Now, Father, I thank You for Your Word, and how Your Word does not return unto You void, but it accomplishes that in which You send it to perform. So as I have prayed Your Word, I thank You that Your blessings are performed and accomplished in my life. In the name of the Lord, Jesus Christ, I pray, AMEN!

*Scriptures Used In This Prayer:*

| | | |
|---|---|---|
| 3 John 1:2 | Deuteronomy 28:2 | Psalms 23:6 |
| Colossians 2:7 | Malachi 3:10 | Psalms 1:3 |
| Colossians 1:23 | Jeremiah 29:11 | Matthew 16:19 |
| Revelation 1:6 | Psalms 35:27 | Ephesians 6:12 |
| Job 22:28 | Revelation 3:8 | 2 Corinthians 10:4-5 |
| Deut. 28:1-13 | Deuteronomy 2:7 | Job 22:28 |
| 2 Timothy 1:7 | Psalms 1:3 | Isaiah 58:6 |
| Philippians 4:7 | Matthew 6:33 | Proverbs 6:30-31 |
| Psalms 23:2 | Psalms 37:4 | Isaiah 55:11 |

# *When You Have A Financial Need*

Father, I come boldly before Your throne of grace that I may obtain help in this time of (financial) need in my life.

You said that we have not because we ask not. So I come before You in prayer, making my request known unto You, and asking for Your provision in supplying this need before me; for You said that if evil men know how to give good gifts unto their children, then how much more will our Heavenly Father give good gifts (and needful things) to His children that ask Him. So I ask through prayer, and by faith in Your unfailing Word for this petition.

Father, You told us in Your Word, that if we would seek first the Kingdom of God and all of Your righteousness, You would bless all of our needs to be added unto us. You also told us that if we would delight ourselves in You, that You would give us the desires of our heart. Father, I pray that You would help and bless me to always seek You and Your righteousness first and foremost in my life; and I pray that I will always find my delight in You; and as I do so, I thank You for supplying every one of my needs, and blessing me with the desires of my heart.

Lord, You are my Shepherd. And as my Shepherd, I confess Your Word that I shall not want (or be in lack of) any good, beneficial or needful thing in my life. For You are the God of my provisions, who supplies all my needs according to Your riches in glory; and You promised that You would not withhold any good thing from Your people who walk upright before You.

Father, You said that Your Spirit runs to and fro throughout the whole earth to show Yourself strong on behalf of those whose hearts are mature towards You; therefore, I thank You for showing Yourself strong unto me against my enemies of debt and lack, and giving me victory over them as You supply this need, as well as every need in my life.

Father, You warned us that we would have many afflictions, but You also promised that You would deliver us from them all. Therefore, I thank You for Your strong hand of deliverance in supplying and meeting this need for me. For Your Word says that You have never forsaken the righteous, nor allowed his seed to beg for bread. And Father, I confess according to Your Word that I am the righteousness of God – not because of my works, but because I am created in Christ Jesus, and I am made righteous through Him.

Father, You have established us as kings and priests unto the Most High King, Jesus Christ; and You said that when a king shall decree a thing, it shall be established. So by Your authority, I decree that this present need in my life is established, and all of my needs are met and fulfilled.

Father, I thank You for the power and the authority You have given unto us to speak to our circumstances. For You said that we can speak to our mountains and command them to be removed and cast into the sea. So Father, by the authority of Your Word, I speak to this mountain of debt, bills, and financial obligations before me. I speak to my *(name Your specific bills or financial obligations)*, and I command them to be uprooted, removed from before me, and cast into the sea.

Father, as Jesus blessed the two fish and five loaves of bread and multiplied them to be able to feed the five thousand and still have plenty left over, I also speak the Word of God to my finances, and I command them to be multiplied to be able to pay all my bills; and I thank You that I still have plenty left over. And, I confess Your Word that I am completely out of debt, and I owe no man anything but to love them.

Father, I thank You for the promise of Your Word that You would rebuke the devourer for my sake. So by Your promise, and by the authority You have given unto me, I bind every hindering spirit that has attacked my finances. I bind every spirit of debt, lack and insufficiency in my life; and by the Word of the living God, I rebuke and cast them down, and I command them to loose and release every hold from my life and my finances, by the power and the authority of the name of Jesus Christ.

Father, according to Your Word, if an enemy is caught stealing, he must return seven-fold of that which he has stolen. Father, I have caught the enemy stealing (from me). For Your Word has revealed and exposed him as the thief that comes to steal, kill and destroy. So Satan, I command you by the authority of God's Word to return everything you have stolen from my life. And, for every "single" thing you have stolen from my life and my finances, I command you to return unto me seven times that amount, by the authority of the name of the Lord, Jesus Christ.

Now Father, I believe Your Word, and I am fully persuaded that what You have promised, You are also able to perform. And this is the confidence that I have: that if I ask anything according to Your will, I know that You hear me; and since I know that You hear me, I know that I have the petitions that I desire and I have asked of You. I believe it, and I receive the blessings of the Lord in my life.

In the name of Jesus Christ, I pray, AMEN!

## *Scriptures Used In This Prayer:*

*Hebrews 4:16*
*James 4:2-3*
*Matthew 7:7-11*
*Mark 11:24*
*Matthew 6:33*
*Psalms 37:4*
*Psalms 23:1*
*Philippians 4:19*
*Psalms 84:11*
*2 Chronicles 16:9*
*Psalms 34:19*
*Jeremiah 32:21*
*Psalms 37:25*
*Titus 3:4-7*

*Ephesians 2:10*
*2 Corinthians 5:21*
*Revelation 1:6*
*Job 22:28*
*Matthew 21:21-22*
*Matthew 14:19-21*
*Romans 13:8*
*Malachi 3:11*
*Matthew 16:19*
*Proverbs 6:30-31*
*John 10:10*
*Romans 4:21*
*1 John 5:14*

# *When You Need The Favor Of God*
### *For Jobs, Court Cases, etc.*

Father, in the name of Jesus Christ, I come boldly before Your throne of grace asking for Your favor in _____.

I thank You Father that my heart is delighted in loving You, serving You, and praising You. And You said in Your Word that if we would delight ourselves in You, that You would give us the desires of our heart. So I thank You for granting me my heart's desire and blessing me with _____.

Father, Your Word says that the heart of man is in Your hands and You can turn man's heart according to Your purpose. Even as the decision for _____ is in the hands of _____, I thank You for touching _____'s heart, granting me favor, and blessing me with _____.

Father, even as You gave Esther favor before the king to be chosen as the queen out of the choice of thousands, I thank You that as my name is considered, that You would give me the same favor before _____ and grant me _____.

Even as David gave Mephibosheth (undeserving) favor because of David's friendship with his father, Jonathan, I thank You for giving me favor with _____ because of my relationship with You, through the shed blood of Jesus Christ.

I thank You that You make all grace abound towards me so that I have all sufficiency in all things. I therefore thank You for Your abounding grace and Your unmerited favor in blessing me with _____.

Father, Your Word says that we have not (what we need or desire) because we ask not. You also said that we do not get what we pray for because we ask amiss (the wrong way). So I ask (not amiss) but in faith, according to Your Word to bless me with _____.

By the authority of the name of Jesus Christ, I bind every demonic spirit, every principality and every spirit of wickedness in high places that would attempt to stop or hinder me from receiving _____. And I also pull down every spirit of doubt, fear, worry and unbelief concerning this petition.

I thank You Father, that You are with me, and therefore Your favor is also with me. For Your Word says that if God be for us, then nothing is able to succeed in stopping us, hindering us, or coming against us.

I release my faith and my confidence in You that as I have asked according to Your will (which is Your Word), then I know that You hear me. And if I know that You hear me, whatsoever I ask (in faith), then I know that I have the petition that I have desired of You.

Now Father, as I have prayed Your Word, I thank You in advance that as I have favor with You (because of Christ), I therefore have favor in this situation. And as I have prayed Your Word, I believe that I have already received _____. And by faith in You, and Your grace and mercy towards me through Christ Jesus, I thank You and praise You for blessing me with _____.

In the name of Jesus Christ, I call it done, AMEN!

## *Scriptures Used In This Prayer:*

*Hebrews 4:16*
*Psalms 37:3*
*Exodus 7:3-5*
*Esther 2:8-17*
*2 Samuel 9:7*
*Psalms 107:2*
*2 Corinthians 9:8*
*Proverbs 12:2*
*James 4:2-3*
*Matthew 16:19*
*Ephesians 6:12*
*2 Corinthians 10:4-5*
*Romans 8:31*
*1 John 5:14-15*

# Chapter VI

## Prayers for Directions — Also for Anger and Help in Troubles

# *For Directions And Instructions*

Father, in the name of Jesus Christ, I come boldly before Your throne of grace asking for divine directions and instructions concerning _____.

Father, I trust not in my own knowledge or wisdom concerning _____, and I lean not to my own understanding. For I realize that my knowledge without You is empty, and my understanding without You is vain. I choose to rather, acknowledge You, O Lord, concerning this matter. For Your Word tells us that if we acknowledge You in all our ways, You would direct our path. So as I acknowledge You in this situation, I thank You for directing me and leading me in Your path.

I thank You that Jesus Christ dwells within me in the person of the Holy Spirit. For You said that in Jesus name, You will send the Holy Spirit, and He shall lead and guide us to all truth. So I thank You for the leading and guidance of the Holy Spirit to Your truth, guidance, and direction concerning this matter.

I thank You Father that You are a lamp unto my feet and a light unto my path; and I praise You for lighting my way. For You also said in Your Word that You would guide me with Your eyes and Your Spirit. So Father, I submit myself unto You, as You lead, guide, and direct me by Your all-seeing eyes and Your ever-knowing Spirit.

Father, Your Word says that the steps of a righteous man are ordered by You, O Lord. I know that I am not righteous in my own works or deeds, but You have made me righteous through the blood of Christ Jesus. So therefore, I thank You for divinely ordering my every step concerning _____.

Lord, You are my Shepherd. So I thank You for being a watchful Shepherd over me, who shall lead me down the right path concerning _____, and for keeping me from straying in the wrong direction.

Father, You said that Your sheep know Your voice, and a stranger they will not follow. I thank You for helping me to ignore the voice of the stranger (Satan), and for helping me to clearly and distinctively hear Your voice (the Great Shepherd) for instructions and directions in this situation; for I know that following Your voice leads to life, liberty and peace; whereas, following the voice of the enemy leads to death, bondage and confusion. So Father, I refuse to follow the voice of the stranger, and I choose to follow only the voice of my Shepherd, Jesus Christ.

By the authority of the name of Jesus Christ, I bind the spirit of deception and every other satanic spirit that would attempt to deceive me or lead me down the wrong path. I cast down every spirit of confusion, and I pull down every stronghold of fear. For You have not given me a spirit of fear (or confusion), but a spirit of power, and of love, and a sound mind.

I thank You Father that just as Joseph told Pharaoh that You would give him an answer of peace concerning the awesome dilemma before him – as I have sought Your face, I thank You for also giving me an answer of peace concerning this matter before me.

Now Father, I cast all my worries, cares and anxieties concerning _____ upon You; and I thank You for sustaining me with Your answer of peace and instructions. And as I have committed this situation unto You, I thank You in advance for Your instructions, guidance and Your clear-cut directions. In the name of Jesus Christ, I Pray, AMEN!

## *Scriptures Used In This Prayer:*

*Hebrews 4:16*       *Psalms 37:23*
*Proverbs 3:5-6*     *2 Corinthians 5:21*
*John 14:26*         *John 10:2-5*
*Psalms 119:105*     *Matthew 16:19*
*Psalms 32:8*        *2 Corinthians 10:4-5*
*Psalms 23:1*        *Genesis 41:16*
*Psalms 23:3*        *Psalms 55:22*
*Jude 1:24*          *Psalms 37:5*

# When You Are Angry

Father, I come boldly before Your throne of grace to find help and deliverance in a time of need from anger.

Father, Your Word tells us that offenses will come. I confess unto You that I have been offended by _____ because of (*name the offense*). I also confess unto You that it has made me angry. Your Word tells us to confess our faults, sins and shortcomings, and You will heal us. So as I confess this anger upon me, and I thank You for Your healing and deliverance from it.

Father, Your Word tells me that when offenses come, and I become angry, to "not" allow the sun to go down upon my wrath or anger – thereby allowing it to infiltrate my heart, and lead to other spirits and sin in my life. So I refuse to give place to the devil to allow him to manifest himself in my life. With my prayer, and the Word and power of the Living God, I cut off this demonic access to my life and my spirit, and I pray, Father, that You would intervene (on my behalf) and deliver me from this anger.

Father, as this offense has lit an explosive fuse of fury in my heart, I'm asking that You would come into my heart with the gentleness and comfort of Your Spirit, and diffuse me. I pray that You would remove the spirit of anger, rage and indignation from my heart, and replace it with the spirit of peace and love. And, may You soothe my heart and give me a calm and quiet spirit.

Father, I thank You for the authority You have given me through Christ Jesus; and with that authority, I bind and loose the spirit of anger from my life. I also bind, loose, and cast down every sinful manifestation of anger in my life, including the spirit of malice, strife, bitterness, wrath, and every other contentious, demonic manifestation of Satan in my life, by the authority of the name of Jesus Christ.

I speak Your Word that greater is He (Jesus Christ) that is in me (who gives me power over anger and its manifestations) than he (Satan) that is in the world, who prompts and attempts to induce me to anger.

Father, through Your deliverance in helping me to rid my heart of anger, I thank You that it closes the door to Satan and demonic hindrances, and opens the door for Your goodness, mercy, grace, favor and Your blessings in my life.

Father, I pray that You would help me not to become hardhearted. When anger attempts to come upon me and overtake me, and You speak to my heart about anger, help me to be open and receptive, and listen to the still, small voice of Your Spirit that brings conviction upon my heart – and through it, repentance, deliverance, and change.

When I am tempted with anger, help me to give a soft answer, which turns away wrath in my heart and in the hearts of others. And help me not to give in to, or be hasty in anger, but use discretion, and be slow to wrath and slow to anger.

Father, I'm asking that You would help me to be an example to my wife/husband, children, family, those upon my job, and others around me by displaying the peace and love of God within me instead of anger. Keep me from reacting to stressful situations and difficult people by exploding, and reacting in anger and with vile, profane or repulsive answers, responses or words. Help me, rather, to display the fruit of the Spirit, by responding in the Spirit of love, with kindness and kind words, gentleness, temperance, meekness and long-suffering.

Now Father, I commit this offense and situation unto You; and I thank You for Your spirit of peace and deliverance in my life. I decree according to Your Word that I am loosed and set free from the spirit of anger, and from any demonic manifestation or hindrance connected to this spirit. For he in whom the Son has set free is free indeed. And as I go forth, I thank You for blessing me to walk in spiritual liberty, and under the influence of Your love, peace and the Holy Spirit in my life.

In the name of Jesus Christ, I pray, AMEN!

## *Scriptures Used In This Prayer:*

| | |
|---|---|
| *Hebrews 4:16* | *Ezekiel 3:7* |
| *James 5:16* | *1 Kings 19:12* |
| *1 John 1:9* | *2 Corinthians 7:10* |
| *Ephesians 4:26* | *Proverbs 15:1* |
| *Ephesians 4:27* | *Proverbs 16:13* |
| *Psalms 18:35* | *Proverbs 16:32* |
| *2 Timothy 1:7* | *Proverbs 19:11* |
| *1 Peter 3:4* | *Ecclesiastes 7:9* |
| *Matthew 16:19* | *1 Timothy 4:12* |
| *Ephesians 6:12* | *Romans 5:5* |
| *2 Corinthians 10:4-5* | *Galatians 5:16* |
| *Isaiah 58:6* | *Galatians 5:22-23* |
| *1 John 4:4* | *John 8:36* |
| *Genesis 4:7* | *Galatians 5:1* |

# *When You Are In Trouble*

Father, I come boldly before Your throne of grace to find help from these troubles that are before me. So I look unto the hills (unto You), from which comes my help. For my help and deliverance comes only from You.

Father, because You are my help, when I am troubled on every side, I know that I am not in distress. When it looks like I am perplexed, because I know that You are with me, I am not in despair. When I am persecuted, I have confidence in Your Word, that I have not been forsaken. And, when it looks like I have been cast down, because of my faith in You, I know that I am not destroyed; because You are my deliverance, and a very present help in times of trouble.

Father, You said that when I am in trouble, I can call upon the name of the Lord, who is my help and my strength, and You will answer me, and deliver me from my troubles. So I call upon You, O Lord, because You are my Strong Tower and my Defense, and I run unto You that I may find safety and shelter. For You are my hiding place, and You preserve me from trouble.

Father, You said that as we go through the waters, You shall be with us, and the waters shall not overtake us. And when we go through the fire, we shall not be burned. As Shadrach, Meshach and Abednego went through the fire and were not burned, nor had the smell of smoke on their clothing, I pray that as I go through this fire of affliction, that You shall go through it with me, and bless me to also come through victoriously as pure gold. For You said that many are the afflictions of the righteous, but You promised to deliver us from them all.

Father, You told Joshua that You did not come to fight with him in his battles, but You came to take over. Therefore, I stand back and allow You, O Lord, to take over and take charge of my battles to bring me to an expected end. And as I allow You to fight this battle for me, I thank You that I shall stand still and see Your salvation and Your strong hand of deliverance.

As Joshua and the people of Israel marched around the walls of Jericho, and shouted, and the walls came down, I thank You that as I pray Your Word, that You would also cause my walls of troubles to fall down from around me as You did the walls of Jericho.

Father, I thank You for the authority You have given to us to speak to our circumstances. So I speak to my mountains, which are these troubles before me, and I command them to be removed, uprooted, and cast into the sea. And as Jesus spoke to the raging winds and the sea, and calmed them with the power of His Word, I also speak the Word of God to my raging sea of troubles, and I command them to *"be at peace, and be still,"* by the authority of the name of Jesus Christ!

Father, I ask that You would search my heart to see if there is any error in my ways concerning these troubles. And if there is error in my ways, I ask that You would forgive me for my actions, create within me a clean heart, and renew a right spirit within me; and according to Your loving kindness and tender mercy, have mercy upon me, O God, and deliver me from these troubles.

I bind every demonic spirit, every principality, and every spiritual wickedness in high places that has launched this attack against my life. I render them helpless, powerless, inoperative and ineffective against me. I pull down every stronghold, and I cast down every work of darkness of the enemy from my life, and from this, as well as every situation in my life, by the authority of the name of Jesus Christ!

I decree according to the Word of the Living God, that this weapon that has been formed against me shall "not" prosper; and every tongue that has risen against me in this attack shall be brought to shame. I also thank You Father for contending with them that contend with me in this trouble, and fighting on my behalf.

As I go through this trouble, I bind worry, doubt, fear, and unbelief. And Father, I rest in Your peace – the peace that passes all understanding; and I pray that You would keep me in Your perfect peace, as You keep my heart and mind stayed upon You.

Father, I know that You are the Sovereign God; and You knew that these troubles would come upon me even before I was born. And because You knew this, I know that You are able to take these things that the devil meant for evil, and turn them around into victory for me. For Your Word says that You cause all things to work together for the good of those who love You. So I put my trust in You – knowing that Your grace is sufficient for me; and I am confident that in the end, I will get the victory, and You will be glorified.

I thank You that as I go through this trial – regardless of the outcome, that these troubles shall not devastate me, nor my faith and trust in You. May You secure and anchor my faith, and cause my faith to be steadfast, unmovable, and deeply rooted and grounded in You.

I speak Your Word that neither this attack against me, nor anything else shall be able to separate me from You, nor my love for You. And I rest in confidence, knowing, that if You are for me, which I know that You are, then nothing is strong enough or able to come against me and succeed.

Now Father, I thank You in advance for my victory and deliverance from these troubles. And I rest in Your peace, knowing that You know how to deliver the righteous from trouble. So in the name of Jesus Christ, I thank You and I give You praise for my victory. AMEN!

## *Scriptures Used In This Prayer:*

| | |
|---|---|
| *Hebrews 4:16* | *Psalms 139:23-24* |
| *Psalms 121:1-8* | *Psalms 51:1* |
| *Psalms 107:6* | *Psalms 51:10* |
| *2 Corinthians 4:8-9* | *Ephesians 6:12* |
| *Psalms 46:1* | *2 Corinthians 10:4-5* |
| *Romans 10:13* | *Job 22:28* |
| *Psalms 91:14-15* | *Isaiah 58:6* |
| *Proverbs 18:10* | *Isaiah 54:17* |
| *Psalms 121:7* | *Isaiah 49:25* |
| *Isaiah 43:1-2* | *Psalms 118:6* |
| *Daniel 3:5-28* | *Philippians 4:7* |
| *Psalms 34:19* | *Isaiah 26:3* |
| *Joshua 5:13-15* | *Romans 8:28* |
| *Jeremiah 29:11* | *Psalms 25:20* |
| *Exodus 14:13* | *2 Corinthians 12:9* |
| *2 Chronicles 20:17* | *Colossians 1:23* |
| *Joshua 6:1-20* | *Psalms 16:8* |
| *Luke 9:1* | *Romans 8:35-39* |
| *Matthew 16:19* | *Romans 8:31* |
| *Mark 4:39* | *2 Peter 2:9* |

# Chapter VII


# Prayers for Deliverance, Forgiveness and Spiritual Strength

# *For Power Over Lust And Sexual Sins*

F ather, I come boldly before Your throne of grace to find help and strength over the spirit of lust in my life.

Father, You told us to watch and pray so that we would not enter into temptation. Therefore, I enter into prayer, seeking Your help so that I will not enter, be drawn, or fall into temptation.

I confess Your Word over my life that I am a new creature in Christ Jesus. The old things in my life are passed away – which includes my old life of sin and lust; and behold, all things have become new – which means I now have a new nature, which is the nature of God; because even though I am in the world, I am not of the world; and because I have the nature of Christ, I will not be controlled by the lusts or the seductions of the world.

I speak Your Word over my life that I am crucified with Christ; and through Christ, the lusts and affections of my flesh have been crucified also; nevertheless, I live; yet it is not I that live, but Jesus Christ who lives in and through me, giving me power over lust and sin; and the life that I now live in the flesh, I live it by the faith, power, and strength of the Lord, Jesus Christ.

Father, as I wake each day, help me to gird the loins of my mind and put on the whole armor of God, so that I will be able to stand against any and all of the wiles, deceptions and seductions of Satan.

I pray that You would help me "not" to give place to the devil in my life, by avoiding the presence and appearance of evil (and temptation). Help me not to go to places that would cause me to be tempted. Help me not to go around people that would cause me to be tempted. Help me not to watch television programs and movies that would cause me to be tempted. Help me not to allow myself to get involved in compromising situations and conversations that would cause me to be tempted. And help me to avoid anything that would draw my heart away into lust, lasciviousness, sexual sins or perversions of any kind.

Father, I put no confidence in my will, strength or ability to withstand the devil and his temptations. I place my confidence and trust only in You and Your ability to keep me from falling. For I realize that my strength is through You and the power of Your Spirit. Therefore, I confess according to Your Word, that *"I AM STRONG IN YOU, O LORD, AND IN THE POWER OF YOUR MIGHT!"*

Father, I thank You for warning us of the strange woman/man. I pray that You would give me the wisdom, power and strength not to be drawn by her/his flattery, eyes, beauty, words, nor any deception that Satan would use to try to draw me to him/her. I thank You for helping me not to be drawn away with the lust of my eyes; for I realize that the eyes are the door to the heart, and You told us to guard our hearts with all diligence. Therefore, I ask that You would help me to guard my heart by the thoughts of my mind and the discipline of my eyes; and help me to keep my eyes, as well as my mind, single, and stayed upon You.

I pray that You would help me to discipline my mind. Help me to think upon things that bring edification and strength to my spirit rather than destruction. And, help me to continually renew my mind in Your Spirit and Your Word, so that I would not be conformed to the world, nor the world's way of thinking, but rather, transformed daily unto the image of Jesus Christ.

Father, I thank You that my spirit takes the oversight of my soul and body and brings them under subjection. I thank You that my body is the temple of the Holy Spirit, and through Your help and strength, I will not defile Your temple with lust or sin in my life.

I pray that You would help me not to be passive or negligent in dealing with the attacks of the enemy in my life in this area. Help me to be sober-minded, vigilant and watchful at all times of the ploys and seductions of the enemy. And, help me to fight continually to keep my mind and body under the influence of Your power and Spirit (rather than the influence of lust), through the confession of Your Word, the discipline of my eyes, and the transformation of my mind unto Jesus Christ.

I thank You for Your power, inspiration and influence to walk in the Spirit. For You said that if we walk in the Spirit, then we shall not fulfill the lust of the flesh. So I pray that You would help me not to walk under the influence of Satan, but rather, in the power, obedience and influence of Your Spirit.

Father, Your Word tells us that when we are tempted, You will always make a way of escape for us. I therefore thank You for making a way of escape for me out of every trap of the enemy through the strength and power of Your Spirit within me. For Your Word says that You know how to lead us out of temptation, keep us from falling, and deliver us from the evil one.

Your Word says that we shall receive power, after that the Holy Ghost is come upon us. I thank You Father for filling me with the power of the Holy Ghost until it overflows. May You keep me filled with a freshness of Your anointing and power from upon high. And as I am anointed, I thank You for giving me the mind, will and power of Your Spirit to resist the devil. For Your Word says that if we resist the devil, he will flee from us.

Father, I thank You for the authority You have given me in Christ Jesus; and with that authority, I bind every demonic spirit, every principality and every spirit of wickedness in high places that is over or upon my life, attempting to lure me to sexual sins. Satan, I bind your power and influence in my life. I pull down every stronghold of lust, fornication, adultery, pornography and lasciviousness. I loose every unclean spirit from my life; and I render each and every one of these spirits to be helpless, powerless, inoperative, and ineffective to operate anywhere in my life, by the authority of the name of Jesus Christ! Satan, you are defeated in my life; you are under my feet; and by the authority of the name of Jesus Christ, your power of lust and sin is broken from my life!

I cast down every wicked, lustful, lascivious, and unclean thought of the devil in the name of Jesus Christ. I dismiss them from my mind; I refuse to take any thoughts of the devil, and I assassinate every evil thought and imagination by the Word of the Living God.

Now Father, I thank You for Your Word, and for establishing Your Word in my heart and in my life; and I know that according to Your Word, I am strong in You, O Lord, and in the power of Your might; and I shall stand strong and victorious over lust, over every sexual sin and temptation, and over every other sin in my life – not by my might, nor by my own power, but by the strength of Your Spirit. So as I have prayed Your Word, I give You all the glory, honor, and the praise, for my victory.

In the name of Jesus Christ, I pray, Amen!

## *Scriptures Used In This Prayer:*

*Hebrews 4:16*

*Matthew 26:41*

*2 Corinthians 5:17*

*John 17:15-18*

*Galatians 2:20*

*1 Peter 1:13*

*Ephesians 6:11*

*Ephesians 4:27*

*Genesis 39:7-12*

*1 Thessalonians 5:22*

*Philippians 3:3*

*Psalms 143:8*

*2 Samuel 22:33*

*Ephesians 6:10*

*Proverbs 2:16*

*Proverbs 5:3-14*

*Proverbs 6:24*

*Proverbs 7:5*

*James 1:14-15*

*2 Timothy 2:26*

*Proverbs 4:23*

*Isaiah 26:3*

*Philippians 4:8*

*Ephesians 4:23*

*Romans 12:2*

*1 Corinthians 6:15-17*

*1 Corinthians 9:27*

*1 Peter 5:8*

*Matthew 26:41*

*Galatians 5:16*

*2 Corinthians 10:5*

*1 Corinthians 10:13*

*1 Corinthians 10:13*

*Matthew 6:13*

*Jude 1:24*

*Acts 1:8*

*Psalms 92:10*

*James 4:7*

*Matthew 16:19*

*Ephesians 6:12*

*Job 22:28*

*Isaiah 58:6*

*2 Corinthians 10:5*

*Ephesians 6:10*

*Zechariah 4:6*

# *When You Need Deliverance From A Problem Or Habit*

Father, I come boldly before Your throne of grace to find help, strength and deliverance in a time of need. You said that if we ask anything according to Your will, that You will hear us and answer us. Father, I know that it is Your will for us to be delivered and walk in the deliverance whereby You have set us free; therefore, I ask that You would deliver me from this problem of _____.

Father, You said in Your Word that You would deliver us from every evil work, and preserve us unto Your heavenly Kingdom. Father, I know that Jesus Christ came and gave us deliverance at Calvary; therefore, knowing that it is Your will for us to be delivered, I know that I have the victory I desire over this problem. For You also said in Your Word that if we ask anything according to Your will, that You would give us the petitions that we desire of You.

I thank You Father for giving me the mind of Christ; and I confess that my mind is controlled by the Holy

Spirit. I thank You that I am not conformed to the world, but I am transformed unto Jesus Christ by the renewing of my mind. I pray that You would help me to gird up the loins of my mind, and bless me to continually wear the whole armor of God, whereby I will not be deceived or taken in by the tricks and deceptions of the enemy.

Father, I stand firm in my place of victory whereby You have set me free. And since You have given me liberty and set me free, I refuse to be further entangled with the yoke of bondage, I lay aside every weight and sin which holds me back, and I run with patience the race that is set before me.

Father, I thank You for the authority You have given us over Satan and his works; and with that authority, I bind every demonic spirit, every principality, and every spiritual wickedness in high places from my life. I render these, and every demonic spirit against my life to be helpless, powerless, inoperative, and ineffective to prosper against me in any way, or to keep me in bondage any longer.

I thank You Father that the weapons of our warfare are not carnal, but mighty through God to the pulling down of strongholds and casting down imaginations. Therefore, by the authority of the Word of the Living God, I pull down this stronghold of _____ in my life. I cast down every wicked imagination over my mind regarding _____, and I cast down every high thing and power of darkness that exalts itself to resist the power of God through me to stop _____. And Satan, I decree that you are under my feet, and your power of _____ in my life is now broken! I decree all these things by the power and the authority of the name of Jesus Christ!

Father, I confess Your Word that I am crucified with Christ, and all the former lusts and affections of my flesh have been crucified also. Nevertheless, I live; yet it is not I that live, but Christ that lives within me, who gives me power over the flesh, and over _____; and the life which I now live in the flesh, I live it by the power, strength, and faith of the Lord, Jesus Christ.

I thank You Father that I am a new creature in Christ; the old things are passed away, and behold, all things have become new in my life. I have a new nature, which is the nature of God.

Father, Your Word says that You have made us to be more than conquerors through Christ Jesus. Therefore, I confess according to Your Word that I am well able to walk in victory, and I am more than a conqueror over _____ because of the strength and power of Christ Jesus that works in and through me.

I thank You Father for Your help – that from this day forward, that I walk in the light and power of my redemption and deliverance which You gave me at Calvary's Cross. And, I decree that I am loosed and set free from _____ and from every power of darkness. For he in whom the Son has set free (through the power of Your Word) is free indeed.

Now Father, I thank You for setting me free and delivering me from every evil work and power of darkness that has held me in bondage concerning _____. I therefore, walk in this liberty, and I stand steadfast and unmovable from my place of victory in Christ. And I now receive my deliverance; for greater is Jesus Christ who lives and dwells within me (who gives me power over _____), than the enemy who is in the world.

In the name of Jesus Christ, I pray, AMEN!

## *Scriptures Used In This Prayer:*

| | |
|---|---|
| *Hebrews 4:16* | *Isaiah 58:6* |
| *1 John 5:15* | *2 Corinthians 10:4-5* |
| *Galatians 5:1* | *Galatians 2:20* |
| *2 Timothy 4:18* | *2 Corinthians 5:17* |
| *1 John 5:4* | *Romans 8:37* |
| *Philippians 2:5* | *Numbers 13:30* |
| *1 Peter 1:13* | *Colossians 1:28* |
| *Romans 12:2* | *Ephesians 3:20* |
| *Ephesians 6:11* | *1 John 1:7* |
| *Ephesians 6:13* | *1 Corinthians 1:30* |
| *Galatians 5:1* | *Luke 4:18* |
| *Hebrews 12:1* | *Colossians 1:13* |
| *Matthew 16:19* | *Galatians 5:1* |
| *Ephesians 6:12* | *1 Corinthians 15:58* |
| *Luke 9:1* | *1 John 4:4* |

# *When You Have Sinned*
### *(And For Power Over Sin And Temptation)*

F ather, I come boldly before Your throne of grace that I may obtain mercy, forgiveness, and deliverance for that which I have done.

I realize that You are the all-seeing and all-knowing God. I know that You saw what I did, and You were even there when I did it. Therefore, I come before You not in the way of Adam. For after Adam sinned, he hid himself, thinking that he could hide from You. Father, I know that I cannot hide my sins from You; and neither do I attempt to hide them – for You know all things. You even know the thoughts and intents of our hearts. Therefore, I stand exposed, naked and open before You, as I confess my sins.

Father, I confess that I have (*name what You have done*). For Your Word says that if we confess our sins before You, that You are a faithful and a just God who will forgive us of our sins, and cleanse us from all of our unrighteousness.

Father, You instructed us in Your Word "not" to forget the benefits that You have given to us as children of God. For You said that You would forgive all our iniquities, and You would heal all our diseases. As I have confessed my sin (s) before You, I therefore thank You for my benefit (through the shed blood of Jesus Christ) of Your mercy and Your forgiveness for that which I have done.

I take authority over Satan, and over every demonic spirit, every principality, and every spiritual wickedness in high places; I bind these, as well as every other evil and demonic spirit from operating in my life, or influencing me to sin in any way, by the authority of the name of Jesus Christ!

Lord, You said that You came not into the world to condemn the world, but that the world through You would be saved. So I bind the spirit of condemnation in my life, and I refuse to be weighed down with condemnation; because I know that he in whom the Son has set free, is free indeed; and Jesus Christ has set me free of this weight of condemnation. Therefore, I refuse to pick it up and carry it again.

Lord, when the woman who was caught in adultery was brought unto You, You told her that You did not condemn her; and I am thankful Father (that as I have repented from my heart), that neither do You condemn me. And as You told her to go, and sin no more, I thank You for Your power, wisdom, and strength of the Holy Spirit that I may go, and sin no more.

I pray that You would break up the fallow ground in my heart, and pull up the roots of sin and iniquity from within me. Change me O God, and do spiritual surgery upon my heart. May You take out the stony heart of rebellion to Your ways, rebellion to Your Word, and rebellion and disobedience to Your Spirit. And may You give me a heart of flesh that is pliable to Your will – one that is receptive, willing and obedient to Your ways and Your Word; and give me, O Lord, a heart that is like Yours.

Father, I thank You that through Jesus Christ, You have delivered us from the power of darkness, and You have translated us into the Kingdom of Your dear Son, Jesus Christ. I thank You that at Calvary, You set me free from Satan's power over me. So from this day forth, I refuse to serve sin, I refuse to yield my members to serve sin, I stand steadfast in the liberty in which Jesus Christ has set me free of the power of sin over me, and I refuse to be further entangled with the sinful yoke of bondage.

Father, I know that I have not obtained perfection yet, so I refuse to dwell upon this mistake that I have made. I put those things behind me; I reach forward to those things that are before me; and I press toward the mark for the prize of the high calling of God in Christ Jesus.

Father, You said in Your Word that the race is not given to the swift nor to the strong. You also said that we must continue to press on and endure to the end. So even though I may have fallen down in the race, I thank You for Your merciful hand to pick me up out of the miry clay of sin, and giving me the power and strength of the Holy Spirit to get back up and continue in the race. For Your Word tells us that a just man may fall many times, but he shall (because of Your grace), rise up again and continue in the race.

I thank You Father for re-establishing me, strengthening me, and filling me with Your joy and gladness. I pray that You would restore unto me the joy of Your salvation. May You create within me a clean heart, and continually renew a right and Godly spirit within me.

I thank You that I am a new creature in Christ Jesus; the old things are passed away – that includes my old life of sin and disobedience unto You; and behold, all things have become new – which means that I now have the nature of God. My nature is no longer to seek and please the flesh, but to seek, please, and do Your perfect will.

Father, I receive Your Word into my heart and my life. And I pray that You would bless me to walk in the Spirit, and hide Your Word deep within my heart, so that I will not sin against You.

Now Father, I thank You for Your mercy and forgiveness. I also thank You for the power that You have given me at Calvary over sin. And I now walk in the light of my redemption through Christ, and I receive Your power and strength into my life, and my victory over sin.

In the name of Jesus Christ, I pray, AMEN!

## *Scriptures Used In This Prayer:*

| | |
|---|---|
| *Hebrews 4:16* | *1 Corinthians 15:58* |
| *Genesis 3:8* | *Galatians 5:1* |
| *Hebrews 4:12* | *Philippians 3:13* |
| *1 John 1:9* | *Philippians 3:14* |
| *Psalms 103:2-5* | *Ecclesiastes 9:11* |
| *Luke 9:1* | *Matthew 24:13* |
| *Matthew 16:19* | *Psalms 40:1-2* |
| *2 Corinthians 10:4-5* | *Proverbs 24:16* |
| *John 3:17* | *Nehemiah 8:10* |
| *Hebrews 12:1* | *Psalms 51:12* |
| *John 8:36* | *Psalms 51:10* |
| *John 8:3-12* | *2 Corinthians 5:17* |
| *Ezekiel 11:18-20* | *Galatians 5:16* |
| *2 Timothy 2:21* | *Psalms 119:11* |
| *Colossians 1:13-14* | *1 Corinthians 1:30* |
| *Acts 26:18* | *1 Chronicles 29:11* |
| *Romans 6:13* | *1 John 5:4* |
| *Romans 6:19* | |

# *Repentance Prayer For A Backslider*

Father, I come boldly before Your throne of grace in the name of the Lord, Jesus Christ, confessing my sins before You as a backslider.

Father, Your Word says that if I confess my sins unto You, that You are faithful and just to forgive me of my sins and cleanse me from all of my unrighteousness. So I confess my sins, iniquities and transgressions unto You. I confess that I have: (*name things You have done*).

I also confess that I have lost my first love (the passion and heart for serving You and obeying Your Word). Father, I ask that You would forgive me for my sins, and forgive me for backsliding and straying away from Your heart and Your presence. And by Your great mercy towards me, I pray that You would cover my sins with the precious blood of Jesus Christ.

Father, I ask that You would create within me a clean heart – one that desires to intimately know You more and draw close unto You at all times. And, may You renew within me a right spirit – one that is lead, controlled and directed by You.

Father, as the eagle's strength is renewed, I ask that You would also renew my strength. May You bless me to become strong in You, and in the power of Your might. And may You restore unto me the joy of Your salvation in serving and loving You more than anything else in my life.

Father, You said in Your Word that a just man may fall many times; but if he would repent, from his heart, You would forgive him and strengthen him to rise again. You also said that the race is not given to the swift, nor the strong, but to the person that would continue to endure to the end. So Father, as I have fallen down in the race, I pray for Your power, Your mind, and Your strength to get back up, now, and continue to press toward the mark (of Christ), and endure to the end.

Now Satan, I denounce you; I denounce your power and influence over me; you are no longer in control of my life; I now choose Jesus Christ to be Lord and Master of my life. By the authority of the name of Jesus Christ, I command you to loose your hands from my life, and loose every demonic influence and stronghold from my life. Satan, I decree that your yoke of sin and control over my life is now broken! And by the power and authority of the name of Jesus Christ, I decree that I am now set free!

Now Father, I commit my life unto You afresh and anew. And I thank You for Your forgiveness, and for Your strength to not only keep me, but to build me in the power of Christ Jesus, and in the strength of Your Spirit. And may You bless my life and help me from this day forth, to walk in victory in Christ, and live a life that is pleasing in Your sight.

In the name of the Lord, Jesus Christ, I pray, AMEN!

## *Scriptures Used In This Prayer:*

*Hebrews 4:16*          *Proverbs 24:16*
*1 John 1:9*            *Acts 26:20*
*Revelation 2:1-4*     *Ecclesiastes 9:11*
*Jeremiah 4:1*         *Matthew 24:13*
*1 Peter 1:18-19*      *Philippians 3:14*
*Psalms 51:10*         *Matthew 6:24*
*Philippians 3:10*     *Matthew 16:19*
*Romans 8:14*          *Isaiah 58:6*
*Isaiah 40:31*         *John 8:36*
*Ephesians 6:10*       *Jude 1:24*
*Psalms 51:12*         *1 John 3:22*

# *When You Need "Spiritual" Strength*

F ather, I come boldly before Your throne of grace to find help and strength in this time of need for spiritual strengthening in my life.

Father, You said, "they that hunger and thirst after You and Your righteousness shall be filled." So I pray that You would cause my soul to hunger and thirst for You, as if I was in a dry and thirsty land where there was no water. As the deer pant for water, may You cause my soul to thirst and pant after You. And Father, as I hunger and thirst after You, I thank You for filling me with Your presence, Your power and Your strength.

Your Word says that the joy of the Lord is my strength. I pray that You would break up the sadness and gloom in my life in living for You and serving You; and fill me with Your joy until it overflows – the kind of joy that is unspeakable and full of glory. For my joy in You, O Lord, is truly my strength.

Father, You said, "they that wait upon You shall be renewed in their strength." Father, I understand that I do not wait on You by doing nothing, but by serving. So I pray that You would help me to serve You with gladness: help me to come before Your presence daily with praise and thanksgiving; give me a new desire and a passion for the reading and studying of Your Word; help me to be disciplined and diligent to speak Your Word and direct my prayers daily unto You; and help me to listen to Your voice for directions and instructions in my life.

As I study Your Word, help me to hide Your Word deep within my heart so that I will not sin against You, nor stray from You or from obedience to Your Word. As I hide Your Word in my heart, may You satisfy my heart with strength, and cause me to be encouraged and renewed. And Father, as You strengthen me, may You cause me to be (spiritually) strong, steadfast and unmovable – like a tree that is planted by the rivers of living waters that cannot and shall not be moved.

As I become diligent in waiting upon (serving) You, I thank You for renewing my spiritual strength. I pray that You would bless me to mount up with wings as eagles, as You lift me up to the spiritual place where I belong. May You bless me to run and not be weary, and walk by the faith, strength, and power of the Holy Ghost, and not faint in my walk with You.

Father, You said for us to stir up the gift that is in us by the laying on of hands; so as I do those things which I know to do, in praying, studying, confessing Your Word, and seeking Your face to know You more, I pray that You would stir up my heart with the fire of God that shall not be quenched by any temptation, trial or attack of the enemy.

Father, as Your love is renewed for us every morning, I pray that You would anoint me with fresh oil, and cause my love for You to be renewed this day, as well as each and every day of my life. And, may You also anoint my heart with a passion to love You and serve You like never before.

Father, draw me near to Your presence where I find my help and strength. Help me not to be satisfied with fellowshipping with You in the outer courts, but help me to come (daily) into the Holy of Holies – into Your secret place, and tabernacle with You in worship, praise and true intimacy. And, as I draw near to You, I thank You for drawing near to me and giving me the strength and encouragement I need to stand and be victorious.

I pray that You would cause me to remember who I am in Christ. For You said that I am the righteousness of God created in Christ Jesus. I pray that You would help me to walk in Your righteousness, and in the light of Your redemption and deliverance which You gave me at Calvary, and keep me from being entangled with the yoke of bondage.

I bind every principality, every demonic spirit, and every spirit of wickedness from my life; and Satan, I command you to loose your hold from every area of my life. I pull down every stronghold; I cast down every wicked imagination; and I render every hindering spirit against me to be helpless, powerless, inoperative, and ineffective. Satan, you are defeated in my life, and I place you under my feet where you belong, by the authority of the name of Jesus Christ!

I cast off every evil work of darkness from my life that has spiritually held me back; I loose the power and influence of sin from my life that has hindered me and my walk with Christ; and by my confession of the Word of God and the power of the Holy Ghost to help me, I lay aside every weight, every sin, and every spiritual hindrance that has beset me, and I run with patience (and the power of God) the race that is set before me.

Father, You said that we can build up ourselves on our most holy faith, by praying in the Spirit. So as I pray in the Spirit, I thank You for building up my spirit-man, and bringing spiritual restoration and strengthening in my life.

Father, You told us that if we are weak, to confess according to Your Word, that we are strong. So I confess according to Your Word, that *"I AM STRONG IN YOU, O LORD, AND IN THE POWER OF YOUR MIGHT!"*

I thank You for giving me the power to walk worthy of the Lord unto all pleasing, being fruitful in every good work, and increasing in the knowledge of God. I thank You therefore that I am strengthened with all might, according to Your glorious power, unto all patience and long-suffering with joyfulness.

I thank You for being the One who renews my strength and restores my soul. I thank You also for leading me in the path of righteousness (and right living) for Your namesake; and I am of good courage, because You have strengthened my heart.

Now Father, as I have spoken Your Word over my life, I receive Your restoration and strength. And I now stand strong in You and in the power of Your might. I also stand strong in Your ability to keep me from falling, and to keep me continually strong, rooted, grounded, settled and established in Your strength. In the name of Jesus Christ, I pray, AMEN!

## *Scriptures Used In This Prayer:*

| | |
|---|---|
| *Hebrews 4:16* | *James 4:8* |
| *Matthew 5:6* | *2 Corinthians 5:21* |
| *Psalms 63:1* | *2 Peter 1:1* |
| *Psalms 42:1* | *Galatians 5:1* |
| *Nehemiah 8:10* | *Matthew 16:19* |
| *Hosea 10:12* | *Luke 9:1* |
| *Psalms 23:5* | *Ephesians 6:12* |
| *1 Peter 1:8* | *2 Corinthians 10:4-5* |
| *Habakkuk 3:19* | *Job 22:28* |
| *Isaiah 40:31* | *Isaiah 58:6* |
| *Psalms 119:11* | *Jude 1:20* |
| *Psalms 103:2-5* | *2 Corinthians 12:10* |
| *Psalms 1:3* | *Ephesians 6:10* |
| *2 Timothy 1:6* | *Colossians 1:10-11* |
| *Lamentations 3:22-23* | *Psalms 23:3* |
| *Psalms 92:10* | *Colossians 1:23* |

# *A Prayer Of The 51st Psalm*

### *A Psalm of Prayer Asking for God's Mercy and Forgiveness*

F ather, I come boldly before You asking for Your mercy and forgiveness for my sins.

I ask according to Your Word that You would have mercy upon me, O God; and according to Your loving kindness, and according to the multitude of Your tender mercies, blot out my transgressions, and forgive me for what I have done.

I pray that You would wash me thoroughly from my iniquity, and cleanse me from my sins. I acknowledge my transgressions and my sins before You. I confess that I have (*name what You have done*). Against You, and You only have I sinned, and have done this evil and wickedness in Your sight. In the secret places of my heart have I hid and conspired this sin.

I pray that You would purge me with hyssop (the precious blood of Jesus Christ), then I shall be clean. Wash me thoroughly from my sins and iniquities – and though my sins be as scarlet, they shall be white as snow. I pray that You would hide Your face from my sins, and blot out all of my transgressions.

May You restore unto me joy and gladness, and the joy of my salvation in You. As You break the bones of rebellion and disobedience in my life, may You restore unto me the joy of loving You and serving You. For it is my joy in You, O Lord, that is my strength.

I pray that You would create within me a clean heart, O God; and may You renew a right, Godly and obedient Spirit within me. Please do not cast me away from Your presence. And by Your grace and mercy, I pray that You would not take Your Spirit or Your anointing from me.

Your Word says that You do not desire sacrifices and burnt offerings for our sins. If this were what You desired, I would gladly give it. But I give unto You what You truly desire of us: I give unto You the sacrifice of a broken spirit and a contrite heart.

As I am changed and converted, not only will I obey Your Word, but I will also teach transgressors Your ways; and through my witness, my testimony and the preaching of Your Word, I shall convert them unto You.

Now Father, for Your forgiveness, and for Your abundant grace, Your bountiful mercy and Your ever-loving kindness towards me, I give You all the praise, honor, glory, adoration and thanksgiving. In the name of Jesus Christ, I pray, and give You thanks, AMEN!

# Chapter VIII

# Prayers of Encouragement and Comfort

# *A Prayer Of The 23rd Psalm*
### *A Psalm of God's Comfort, Peace And Provisions*

O Lord, my God, You are my Shepherd. And because You are, all of my needs are fully supplied and met, and I do not want or lack for any needful thing in my life.

Because You are my Shepherd – the one who loves and cares for me, You not only provide what I need, You also make me to lie down in the green pastures of Your blessings of abundance in every area of my life – spiritually, physically, financially and socially.

No matter what difficulties I face in life, and no matter what problems I go through, You are always with me, leading me besides the still waters of Your peace, rest and security.

Lord, You are the restorer of my soul. When I am weak, You give me strength and make me strong; when I am hurt, downtrodden or bewildered, You encourage my soul and pick me up; and when I am sad or lonely, You comfort me and give me joy.

When the enemy lures me, or I stray away from You down a path of temptation and sin, You lead me to repentance, and back to the correct path of Your righteousness (right living) and obedience to Your Word, for Your namesake.

Even when I go through valleys in my life of dangers, toils and trials, or I face the threat of calamity, disaster or the shadow of death itself, I will command my soul not to fear. And through Your faith, strength and comfort, I will fear no evil, nor will I be worried or afraid, because I will have confidence that You are with me. And as my Great Shepherd, You will never leave nor forsake me, and You will always see me through.

I receive You, O Lord, as my Shepherd – the One who leads me, comforts me and guide me. But I also open my heart to You, and I receive You as the "Bishop" of my soul. For with Your rod of correction and Your staff of authority, You bring correction to my soul because You love me. For You are the One who reproves me, rebukes me, chastise me, and correct me through the inspiration of Your Spirit, and the convicting power of Your Word.

Because You are my Shepherd, when my enemies come against me and try to bring destruction, You are always there to make provisions for me. You prepare a table of blessings for me in the presence of those who are against me, and those who hate me without a cause. And, You even cause them to turn around and bless me.

You fill me with Your power, Your presence and Your anointing; and it breaks and destroys every yoke of the devil in my life, and in the lives of others. Like oil poured into a cup, You pour Your anointing in me until I am filled, running over, and it is overflowing all around me.

You are a faithful God – a faithful Shepherd over my life. And because of Your faithfulness, I have a surety that Your goodness, mercy, loving kindness and Your abounding love shall follow me all the days of my life.

And I shall dwell and abide in You, in Your presence, and under Your arms of comfort, peace and provisions, both now and forever, AMEN!

## *Scriptures Used In This Prayer:*

### *Psalms Chapter 23*

# *When You Are Depressed, Discouraged Or In Despair*

Father, I come boldly before You asking for Your encouragement and Your help to lift me up from this place of despair.

Father, You said that when I am burdened or heavy laden, to come unto You, and You will give me rest and peace unto my soul. So I come unto to You with my burden, asking for Your rest, peace and encouragement.

Father, *(name what has discouraged You)* has saddened my heart and caused me to be discouraged; so I call upon You for my help and my strength; for You are able to deliver my soul. You are the lifter of my head, and the One who is able to lift me up and bring me out.

Your Word says that You turn our mourning into dancing. I thank You for changing my heart from sadness and gloom, into joy, laughter and dancing. May You fill me with Your joy and Your laughter – which is healing, health and medicine unto my soul. For my joy in You,

O Lord, is my strength and my healing.

I pray that You would bring me up and out of this miry clay of depression, and plant my feet upon high, like hinds' feet in high places.

Instead of allowing this spirit of discouragement to keep me down, I choose to take off the garment of discouragement and put on the garment of praise for this spirit of heaviness. So Father, I lift You up, and I magnify You and I praise Your holy name. I confess that You, and You alone are Lord. Regardless of the outcome of this situation, You are still Lord, You have always been Lord, and You shall forever be Lord of all, in all, through all, and above all!

Father, I pray that You would not allow this situation to make me bitter, resentful or angry against You. I pray that You would neither allow it to devastate me or my faith and trust in You. But may You help me, and keep my faith in You strong, steadfast and unmovable. And, may You help me to continue to trust in You even more.

I pray that You would bless me to wait upon You (for my strength) by continuing to serve You (in coming to church, and reading, studying and confessing Your Word). For You said in Your Word that as we wait upon You, O Lord, that You would renew our strength.

Father, I cast all of my cares, worries and discouragement concerning _____ upon You. I pray that You would lift me up from this heavy heart of depression and despair.

As I cast them upon You, I thank You for causing my heart to become lighten, and turning this heaviness into encouragement, determination and hope for Your will, purpose and Your plan for the future for my life.

As You turn and change my heart from despair, may You also change my countenance. As people look upon me, may they not see despair and hopelessness on my face, but rather the reflection of Your bountiful hope, and Your joy and peace that You have placed in my heart.

Father, I thank You for restoring my soul from this spirit of heaviness, and for lifting me up and leading me in Your path of righteousness and encouragement for Your namesake. And I pray that I would not allow this, nor anything else to separate my love from You, nor my service and obedience unto You.

Father, I thank You for the authority You have given me in the name of Jesus Christ; and with that authority, I bind this spirit of discouragement, depression and heaviness from my life. I pull them down from my mind, and I cast them down from my heart. I loose them from my life, and I render these, and every other demonic spirit against me to be helpless and powerless to rest upon me or come against me in any way, by the power and the authority of the name of Jesus Christ.

I thank You Father for blessing me to stand in the liberty whereby Jesus Christ has set me free from every spirit of oppression and depression, and I refuse to be entangled any longer with this yoke of bondage.

Father, I acknowledge that no matter what I have lost, no matter how I have failed, and no matter what I am without – if I have You, then I have everything. For I would rather have Jesus, and my joy in Him, than all the silver, gold and riches of the world without Him. For in Your presence is the fullness of joy; and at Your right hand is where I find my strength, my blessings, my provisions, and my pleasures forever more.

I thank You for redeeming me by the blood of the Lamb. And, You said for us to *"let the redeemed of the Lord, say so."* Father, I confess that I am the redeemed, and I *"say so"* that I am strengthened, encouraged, delivered and set free from every spirit of heaviness and spiritual bondage, by the authority of the name of Jesus Christ.

Father, as David encouraged his heart and continued in You to become victorious. I pray that as I have prayed Your Word, that You would also encourage and lift my heart, as You sustain me in Your might and Your victory.

Now Father, as I have cast this burden of hurt and discouragement upon You, I thank You for anointing me and overshadowing me with Your strength and Your joy. For greater is Jesus Christ who is in me – who is my strength, my joy, and the lifter of my head, than the enemy who is in the world.

In the name of Jesus Christ, I pray, AMEN.

## *Scriptures Used In This Prayer:*

| | |
|---|---|
| *Hebrews 4:16* | *Numbers 6:24-26* |
| *Matthew 11:28* | *Psalms 23:3* |
| *Romans 10:13* | *Romans 8:35-39* |
| *Psalms 23:3* | *Matthew 16:19* |
| *Psalms 27:1* | *Ephesians 6:12* |
| *Psalms 46:1* | *2 Corinthians 10:4-5* |
| *Psalms 3:3* | *Job 22:28* |
| *Psalms 30:11* | *Isaiah 58:6* |
| *Proverbs 17:22* | *Luke 9:1* |
| *Nehemiah 8:10* | *Galatians 5:1* |
| *Psalms 40:2-3* | *Matthew 16:26* |
| *Isaiah 61:3* | *Proverbs 22:1* |
| *Acts 10:36* | *Psalms 16:11* |
| *1 Corinthians 15:58* | *Psalms 107:2* |
| *Isaiah 40:31* | *1 Samuel 30:6* |
| *Psalms 55:22* | |

# *When You Have Been Extremely Hurt or Disappointed*

Father, I come boldly before Your throne of grace that I may find and obtain help, strength, and encouragement in a time of need.

Father, I confess that I have been hurt/disappointed because of (*what happened*). But I know that in times like these, I can look unto You for my help. For Your Word says that You are a very present help in times of trouble, and I can run unto You (in prayer) where there is safety and strength.

I first of all ask according to Your Word for forgiveness for (*person who offended You*) for (*name the offense*). For Your Word commands us to forgive those who sin and trespass against us. Therefore, in obedience to Your Word, I ask for Your forgiveness for _____ for this offense. By the words of my mouth and the obedience of my heart, I release _____ from this transgression, and ask that You would not hold this offense against him.

Father, You instructed us that if we become burdened or afflicted, to cast our cares and burdens upon You, and You would sustain us, because You care for us. So Father, I cast my cares, anxieties and burdens concerning this offense upon You; and I ask that You would sustain my mind and my heart through the frustration, confusion, hurt, disappointment and anguish this offense had caused.

I thank You for our Lord, Jesus Christ, who went to Calvary's Cross and carried all of our sins and our burdens – thus providing for us, *"The Great Exchange."* Father, I exchange my heaviness and burdens for Your yoke. For You instructed us to take Your yoke, which You said is easy, and to also take Your burdens, which are light. Therefore, I give You my cares and worries in exchange for Your yoke of peace. I give You my hurts and disappointments in exchange for Your yoke of healing. I give You my heavy burdens in exchange for Your yoke of rest. And I give You my anxieties in exchange for Your yoke of comfort.

Your Word says that You came to heal the broken hearted and bind up our wounds. You also said that many are the afflictions of the righteous, but You would heal and deliver us from them all. So Father, even as my heart has been wounded from this hurt/disappointment, I thank You for the healing power of Your Spirit in mending my heart and my mind from the wound of this affliction. I thank You also for delivering and healing me from the mental, as well as emotional pain and scars of this hurt/disappointment.

Father, You instructed us in Your Word not to allow anything to separate us from the love of God that is in Christ Jesus. So I pray that You would strengthen my heart and my love for You, that neither this hurt/ disappointment, nor anything else shall be able to separate me from the love of God that is in Christ Jesus, our Lord. I pray for Your help that this affliction will not make me bitter against You, but better, in serving You and continuing to trust in You. And I pray that it will not devastate me, nor my faith in You, but rather, elevate my faith and my walk in You and in Your Word.

I thank You for giving me Your peace in the midst of the valley of this affliction. For You said that You would keep us in perfect peace, as we keep our minds and hearts stayed upon You. Father, I pray that You would not allow my mind to be consumed with this affliction, but rather, help me to keep the loins of my mind girded up in Christ, and thereby in Your perfect peace – the peace that passes all understanding.

Father, I thank You for the authority You have given me in Christ Jesus; and with that authority, I bind every spirit of worry, doubt, fear, depression, oppression, and any other spirit that the enemy would try to put on me as a result of this adversity. I loose them from my mind and my heart; and I render these, as well as every other demonic attack against me to be helpless, powerless, inoperative, and ineffective, by the authority of the name of Jesus Christ!

Father, Your Word says that You are the lifter of our heads, and our joy and gladness in times of sorrow. I thank You therefore that as You renew the strength of the eagle, that You would cause my head to be uplifted, and my joy and gladness renewed and restored, through the strength of Your Spirit and the power of Your Word.

Now Father, I thank You for Your promise to restore my soul. So as I have prayed and spoken Your Word, I thank You for healing and restoration from this hurt/disappointment, and for giving me the strength, joy, and encouragement I need to continue in victory through Christ Jesus, our Lord.

In the name of the Lord, Jesus Christ, I pray, AMEN!

## *Scriptures Used In This Prayer:*

| | |
|---|---|
| *Hebrews 4:16* | *Psalms 23:4* |
| *Psalms 121:1-2* | *Isaiah 26:3* |
| *Deuteronomy 12:10* | *1 Peter 1:13* |
| *Psalms 46:1* | *Philippians 4:7* |
| *Psalms 61:1-3* | *Matthew 16:19* |
| *Psalms 68:35* | *Ephesians 6:12* |
| *Matthew 5:44* | *2 Corinthians 10:4-5* |
| *Matthew 6:15* | *Job 22:28* |
| *Luke 23:34* | *Isaiah 58:6* |
| *Psalms 55:22* | *Psalms 3:3* |
| *Isaiah 53:5* | *Isaiah 35:10* |
| *Matthew 11:28-30* | *Isaiah 40:31* |
| *Psalms 147:3* | *Psalms 23:3* |
| *Romans 8:35-39* | *1 Corinthians 15:57* |

# *For Persecution:*

## *(When You Have Been Lied On, Talked About, or Falsely Accused)*

Father I come boldly before Your throne of grace that I may find help in a time of trouble (from  this attack of persecution upon my life).

Father, I am being *(name the kind of persecution)*. And to my knowledge, I have done nothing to deserve it. But according to Your Word, by faith, I count it all joy; because I know that if they lied on, talked about and falsely accused Jesus, then they will also do the same to me.

First of all, I ask that You would search my heart to see if there is any error in my ways concerning this situation. If there is an error in my ways, I ask that You would reveal it to me, help me to correct my error, and deliver me from it. If there is no error in my ways concerning this problem before me, I thank You for being my Great Advocate and delivering me from this persecution.

I thank You for being my God who fights my battles for me. For Your Word says that the battle is not mine, but Yours. You also said that You did not come to take sides, but to take over. So Father, I stand aside and I allow You to take over this battle and fight on my behalf. I thank You that as I stand still and depend upon You to fight this battle for me, that I shall see my deliverance, and see the salvation of the Lord.

Father, You instructed us in Your Word to forgive those who do us wrong, and pray for those who persecute and despitefully use us. So I ask that You would have mercy upon those who have (*name what they have done*). I pray, by Your mercy and grace, that You would forgive them, and not hold this charge or transgression against them. As I have released them with my words, help me to truly forgive and release them in my heart. And Father, as I have obeyed Your Word to forgive them, I thank You for also forgiving me for all of my transgressions, iniquities and sins.

Father even though it is people who have come against me, I know that it is not the people, but Satan behind the scenes instigating and influencing them. For Your Word tells us that we wrestle not against flesh and blood, but against principalities, against powers, against the rulers of darkness of this world, and against spiritual wickedness in high places. So I speak to each of these spirits behind this attack, and I decree that You *"get thee behind me!"* I bind and loose every demonic spirit of darkness that is promoting and launching this attack against me through these people. Satan, I command you to loose your hold and influence from them, and loose your hands from this situation, by the authority of the name of Jesus Christ.

Father, as Jesus rebuked the (hindering) spirit that was behind Peter, but yet still loved Peter as a person, help me, that as I have rebuked the spirits behind this attack, to be able to look beyond the faults of the people, see their need for prayer, and still love them.

You said in Your Word that no weapon that is formed against me shall prosper, and every tongue that rises against me shall be condemned. I therefore speak Your Word that this weapon cannot and shall not prosper against me; and every tongue that has risen up against me in lies, gossip, and false accusations shall be exposed and brought to an open shame. For Your Word says that You contend with them that contend with me and You fight on my behalf.

Now Father, as I go through this storm of persecution, I thank You for blessing me to rest and abide in Your secret place, under the shadow of Your wings, where there is peace, serenity, rest and security. Help me each day to walk in Your peace – the peace that shall pass the understanding of all those who are against me.

By the authority of Your Word, I cast down every spirit of fear and intimidation of the enemy. For You have not given me a spirit of fear, but a spirit of power and of love, and the sound mind of Christ. I thank You that this attack shall not devastate me, my faith in You, nor my walk in You; but as I look unto You from which comes my help, I thank You for strengthening me and elevating my faith and determination to live for and trust in You even more.

Father, even in the midst of this attack, help me to continue to set my heart, aspiration, and my love upon You. For Your Word says that because I have set my love upon You, that You shall be with me in the midst of trouble, and deliver me from the snare and attacks of the enemy. Your Word also says that You cause all things to work together for the good of those who love You. So as the enemy has set this attack against me, I thank You for turning it around, causing it to backfire on the devil, and work out for my good and for Your glory.

Now Father, I thank You for being my refuge, my fortress, my buckler, my high tower, my victor, and my strength against the enemy. And I thank You in advance for my vindication, and for exposing the truth in this situation. As You expose the truth, may You also expose the devil for who and what he is (a liar, and the father of all lies) – making him an open shame. So I thank You for showing Yourself strong in this fight for me, and for Your mighty hand of power and deliverance on my behalf.

In the name of the Lord, Jesus Christ, I pray, AMEN!

## *Scriptures Used In This Prayer:*

*Hebrews 4:16*  
*Psalms 139:23-24*  
*1 John 2:1*  
*2 Chronicles 20:15*  
*Joshua 5:13*  
*Joshua 5:14*  
*Exodus 14:13*  
*Matthew 6:12*  
*Matthew 6:14-15*  
*Matthew 5:44*  
*Luke 23:34*  
*Ephesians 6:12*  
*Matthew 16:23*  
*Matthew 16:19*  
*Ephesians 6:12*  

*2 Corinthians 10:4-5*  
*Job 22:28*  
*Isaiah 58:6*  
*Isaiah 54:17*  
*Isaiah 49:25*  
*Psalms 91:1*  
*Psalms 17:8*  
*Philippians 4:7*  
*2 Timothy 1:7*  
*Psalms 121:1-2*  
*Psalms 91:14*  
*Romans 8:28*  
*John 8:32*  
*John 8:44*

# *About The Author*

Evangelist Kenneth Scott is the founder and president of Spiritual Warfare Ministries. He is also the author of the much sought after prayer handbook series, entitled, *"The Weapons of our Warfare."* He gave his life to Jesus at the young age of 19 while serving in the United States Army. He served 13 years in the army as a medical combat paramedic, where he learned strategic tactical warfare. It was in learning about the military's strategies and warfare that God used in helping him to understand the spiritual strategies of our warfare with Satan.

In 1990 God called him out of the military into full-time ministry. As he began to serve in ministry as an assistant pastor and church administrator, he realized that the only way he could be effective in ministry was to also be effective in prayer.

Although he had been born again for many years, he realized that his prayer life was not developed enough to pray for and intercede on behalf of the people of God. His cry to the Lord was the same as Jesus' disciples in Luke 11:1 when they asked Him, *"...Lord, teach us to pray, as John also taught his disciples."* Although he found many books on prayer, none of them grasped the power, fire and fierceness of prayer in which he had begun to hunger.

It was then that God led him on a two-year quest gathering the right scriptures and learning more about prayer and the strategies of prayer. In 1992 the Lord lead him to put them into a book entitled *"The Weapons of Our Warfare."* Now, several years later, it has become one of the most sought after Christian books in Christian bookstores and churches.

Tens of thousands have had this same hunger for prayer as Evangelist Scott. And, through the use of this dynamic and powerful prayer handbook, they have learned how to pray the Word of God, put the devil where he belongs in their lives (under their feet), and become developed, armed warriors for Christ.

He now serves the body of Christ as an evangelist, and travels with his wife, Doris, teaching God's people about prayer, and the power and strategies of prayer warfare.

Take advantage of this ministry gift of God to the body of Christ by obtaining books and cassette tape teachings of Evangelist Kenneth Scott. And, prepare yourself for battle, as you experience *"The Weapons of our Warfare, Volumes I and II."*

# About "Spiritual Warfare Ministries"

**S***piritual Warfare Minis-tries* is an intercessory prayer and teaching ministry assisting the body of Christ through teaching the effective, fervent warfare of Prayer. Their desire is to help teach and train believers and Prayer Warriors in the Kingdom of God to be more victorious and availing in their every day walk with the Lord, Jesus Christ through prayer.

In Hosea 4:6 God said, *"my people are destroyed because of a lack of knowledge."* We believe that it's a lack of knowledge of how to strategically use and pray the authority of God's Word in prayer warfare that causes the failure and destruction of many Christian lives.

God has anointed Evangelist Scott to teach God's

people this knowledge through teaching them the proper principles, rules and precepts of prayer. Evangelist Scott teaches the believer how to pray spiritually aggressive prayer, according to God's Word, which enables them to obtain victory in their lives and gives them the knowledge, authority and boldness to take back as well as maintain those things that Satan has stolen from them.

Evangelist Scott and his wife, Doris, have been married for 16 years. They work together in ministry and they both have the same heart and passion for prayer, intercession and the desire to see God's people delivered, set free and loosed from the strongholds and clutches of Satan.

We invite you to take advantage of the ministry teaching and preaching of Author and Evangelist Kenneth Scott. You may contact him at the information on the last page. As you hear him speak under the authority and anointing of the Holy Spirit, your life will never be the same again.

*\* Note: You may also take advantage of the Spiritual Warfare Ministries monthly newsletter, containing enlightening news and information about prayer and other topics that will bless your life. If interested, contact us at the information on the last page.*

# Other Books And Materials By Kenneth Scott

## The Weapons Of Our Warfare, Volume II
If You have enjoyed Volume I, then you need volume II. It is a sequel of volume I, and brings the prayer warrior into the ministry is intercession. A list of prayers that are included in volume I can be found in this enclosure.

## The Weapons Of Our Warfare, Spanish Edition
These are the same anointed prayers as found in the regular version of The Weapons Of Our Warfare, only translated in Spanish. *Coming in July 2001*

## The Keys To The Kingdom
The Keys To The Kingdom is a wealth of scriptures to aid and assist the believer in finding the right scriptures for prayer, study and meditation for just about any situation. *Coming in May, 2001*

## Understanding The Lord's Prayer
Just about all of us have prayed "The Lord's Prayer," and even know The Lord's prayer by memory. But very few of us really understand the depths of what Jesus was truly teaching His disciples in this prayer outline. This book gives the believer a scripture by scripture breakdown of this prayer and gives illumination and insight on its understanding. *Coming in June, 2001*

## The Principles of Prayer:
Jesus said that we have not (what we are praying for) because we ask not. He also said that some of us do ask (in prayer) but we "ask amiss" (the wrong way). There is a right way and a wrong way to pray. This book gives the believer the proper principles and precepts of prayer according to scripture so that your prayers may become effective and strike the mark for what you are praying. *Coming June, 2001*

## Standing In The Gap

This book teaches the believer the ministry of intercession. As Christians, interceding for one another is not a choice, but a commandment. In fact, if we fail to do so, it is actually a sin. Find out more about our role as intercessors, making up the hedge and standing in the gap for others.
*Coming in July, 2001*

## When All Hell Breaks Loose

Most mature Christians can survive the casual trial here and there, but many of God's people fall durring the storms of life. Get this book and learn how to stand through the storm *"When all Hell Breaks Loose."*
Coming in June, 2001

## The Weapons Of Our Warfare
## on Audio Cassette Tapes

Meditate on the anointed Word of God as it is prayed on audio cassette tapes. These tapes contain the same prayers that are in volumes I and II of The Weapons of Our Warfare. As You hear these prayers prayed, you can stand in the spirit of agreement and apply them in the spirit to your life, situations and circumstances as you ride in your car, or as you sit in your home. These tapes are a must for every Christian library.
*Coming in April, 2001*

## Cassette Taped Messages

We have inspiring, powerful and anointed cassette taped messages of Evangelist Scott. To request a catalog of available messages, please write or call.

These products are not all available in bookstores, to order, please contact us at the information on the last page.

# _Prayers In Volume II_

_For the Body of Christ_
_For Unity in the Body of Christ_
_For the Will of God in the Earth_
_For your Pastor_
_For your Church_
_For Members of your Church_
_For Church Services or a Special Service_
_For our Youth_
_For your City_
_For our Nation_
_For those in Authority_
_For Someone that has Lost a Loved One_
_For Someone Needing Deliverance from Drugs_
_For Someone in Prison_
_For Someone to Receive Salvation_
_Introduction: The Need for Salvation_
_A Sinner's Prayer_
_For A Backslider_
_To be an Effective Soul Winner_
_When you Need to Release Forgiveness_
_For Your Tithes and Offerings_
_Introduction: Negative Words and Confessions_
_For Negative Words and Confessions_
_When you Need To Confront Someone_
_For a Single Christian_
_For a Single Christian Woman Desiring A Husband_
_For a Single Christian Man Desiring A Wife_
_For your Job_
_A Supervisor Praying for your Department_
_For your Business_
_For Meetings_

# Contact Us:

For prayer requests, questions or comments, write to:

**Spiritual Warfare Ministries**
**Attention: Kenneth Scott**
**P.O. Box 2024**
**Birmingham, Alabama 35201-2024**

**(205) 853-9509**

**email us at sprwarfare@aol.com**

If there is a specific written prayer which is not included in either volume of this book, that you would like Evangelist Scott to prepare for you, please contact us at the above information.

This Book is not available in all bookstores. To order additional copies of this book, please send 8.99 plus 1.80 shipping and handling to the above address. Please note the volume you are requesting. Bulk quantities may be ordered at reduced rates.

God has anointed Evangelist Scott to teach and preach on the power of prayer. If you are interested in him coming to minister at your church or organization, please contact him at the information above.